Read *With* Me Bible
An NIrV™ Story Bible for Children

Presented to: _____

By: _____

On: _____

Read With Me Bible
An NIrV™ Story Bible for Children

ILLUSTRATED BY

Dennis Jones

EDITED BY

Doris Rikkers and Jean E. Syswerda

ZondervanPublishingHouse
Grand Rapids, Michigan 49530

Published by Zondervan Publishing House
Grand Rapids, MI 49530, U.S.A.
http://www.zondervan.com
Printed in the United States of America
All rights reserved

98 99 00 01 02   12 11 10 9 8 7 6 5 4 3

A special thank-you to Nancy Bordewyk for the initial
work on these Bible story selections as they appeared
in the New International Version. A special thank-you
to Sarah Hupp for the adaptation of this material to
the New International Reader's Version.

Contents

NEW TESTAMENT

OLD
TESTAMENT

The World Begins

Genesis 1

In the beginning, God created
the heavens and the earth.
God said, "Let there be light."
And there was light.

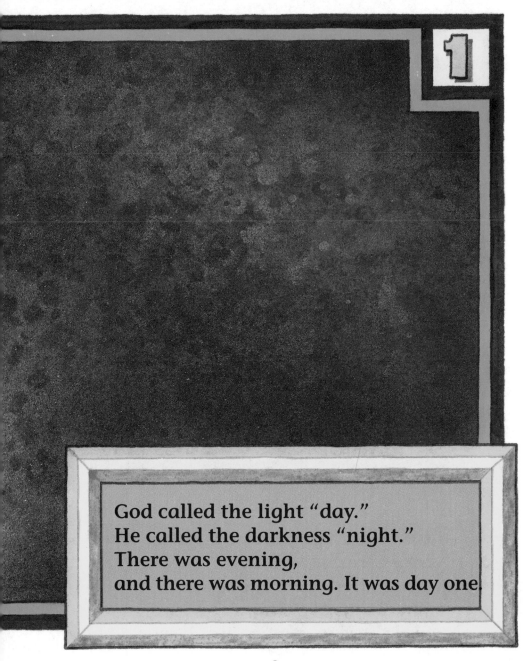

God called the light "day."
He called the darkness "night."
There was evening,
and there was morning. It was day one.

God said, "Let there be a huge space
between the waters."
God called the huge space "sky."
There was evening,
and there was morning. It was day two.

God said, "Let dry ground appear."
Then God said, "Let the land grow plants.
And let there be trees on the land."
And there was evening,
and there was morning. It was day three.

God said, "Let there be lights
in the huge space of the sky."
God made two great lights.
He made the larger light to rule over the day
and the smaller light to rule over the night.
He also made the stars.
And there was evening,
and there was morning. It was day four.

God said, "Let the waters
be filled with living things.
Let birds fly in the sky."
There was evening,
and there was morning. It was day five.

God said, "Let the land
produce living creatures."
And that's exactly what happened.
Then God said, "Let us make man
in our likeness." So God created
man in his own likeness.

God saw everything he had made.
And it was very good.
There was evening,
and there was morning. It was day six.
On the seventh day God rested.

The Garden of Eden

Genesis 2

God planted a garden in Eden.
God made all kinds of trees grow.
Their fruit was good to eat.
The tree that gives life forever
was in the middle of the garden.
The tree that gives the ability to know
about good and evil was also there.

God put Adam in the garden.
He put him there to take care of it.
God brought all the wild animals
and birds to the man to see
what names he would give them.
So the man gave names to all
of the birds and wild animals.

God said, "You can eat the fruit
of any tree in the garden.
But you must not eat the fruit
of the tree of the knowledge of good and evil.
If you do, you will die."

Adam and Eve

Genesis 2

God said, "It is not good
for the man to be alone.
I will make a helper for him."
So God made Adam fall asleep.
God took out one of his ribs.
God made a woman from the rib.
Adam named his wife Eve.

Adam and Eve Fall Into Sin

Genesis 3

The serpent was more clever
than any of the wild animals.
The serpent said to Eve, "Did God
really say that you must not eat the
fruit of any tree in the garden?"
Eve said, "We can eat the fruit
of the trees that are in the garden.

But God did say, 'You must not eat
from the tree in the middle of the garden.
Do not touch it. If you do, you will die.'"
"You won't die," the serpent said.
"God knows when you eat the fruit you will
know things you have never known before.
You will be like God."

Eve took some fruit and ate it.
She gave some to Adam. And he ate it.

Then they realized they were naked.
They sewed fig leaves together
and made clothes for themselves.
They hid from God among the trees.

It was the coolest time of the day.
God called out to Adam, "Where are you?"
"I heard you in the garden," Adam answered.
"I was afraid. I was naked, so I hid."
God said, "Who told you that you were naked?
Have you eaten the fruit of the tree
I commanded you not to eat?"

Adam said, "Eve gave me some fruit
from the tree. And I ate it."
God said to Eve, "What have you done?"
Eve said, "The serpent tricked me.
That's why I ate the fruit."
So God drove them out of the Garden of Eden.

Cain and Abel

Genesis 4

Eve gave birth to Cain and Abel.
Abel took care of sheep.
Cain worked the ground.

Cain gave some things he had grown as an offering to the LORD. Abel brought some lambs. The LORD was pleased with Abel and his offering. But he wasn't pleased with Cain and his offering. So Cain became very angry.

Cain said to his brother Abel,
"Let's go out to the field."
There Cain attacked Abel
and killed him.

Then the LORD said to Cain,
"Where is your brother Abel?"
"I don't know," he replied.
"Am I supposed to look after my
brother?"
So Cain went away from the LORD.
He lived in the land of Nod.

23

Noah's Ark

Genesis 6 — 7

Noah was a godly man.
He walked with God.

The earth was very sinful in God's eyes.
God said to Noah, "I am going to put an end to all
people. I am going to destroy them and the earth.
Make yourself an ark.

Bring male and female
of every living thing into the ark.
Take food for you and for them.
Store it away."

Noah did everything exactly as God commanded.

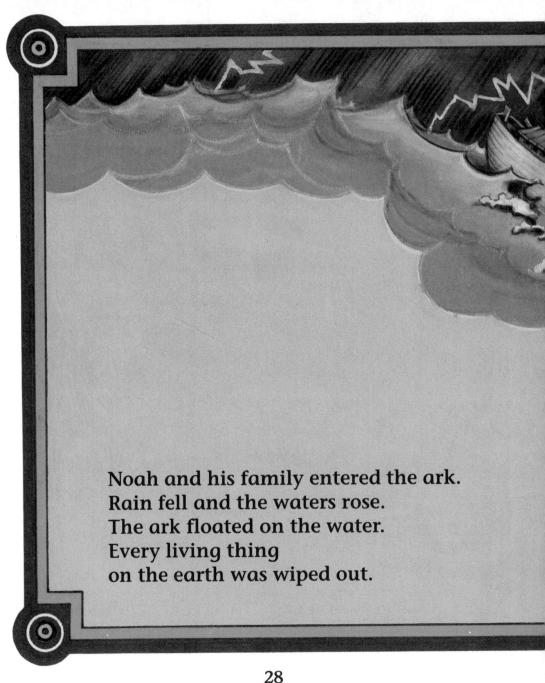

Noah and his family entered the ark.
Rain fell and the waters rose.
The ark floated on the water.
Every living thing
on the earth was wiped out.

Only Noah and those who were
with him in the ark were left.

God's Promise to Noah

Genesis 7 — 8

The waters flooded the earth for 150 days.
But God showed concern for Noah
and all of the animals in the ark.
God sent a wind over the earth.
And the water began to go down.
The ark came to rest on the mountains.

After 40 days Noah opened the window.

Noah sent a raven out.
It kept flying back and forth.

Then Noah sent a dove out.

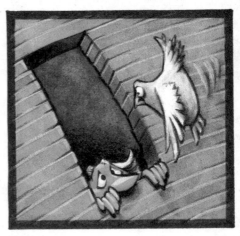

The dove couldn't find any
place to put its feet down.

So the dove returned to Noah.

Noah waited seven more days.
He sent the dove out again.
The dove returned to him.
There in its beak was a fresh olive leaf!
Noah waited seven more days.
He sent the dove out again.
But that time it didn't return to him.

Noah and his family came out of the ark.
All of the animals came out of the ark.
So did all of the birds.
God said, "I will never destroy
all living things again.

As long as the earth lasts,
there will always be a time to plant
and a time to gather crops.
There will always be cold and heat.
There will always be summer and winter,
day and night.
I have put my rainbow in the clouds.
It will be the sign of the covenant between
me and the earth."

35

The Tower of Babel

Genesis 11

The whole world had only one language.
The men said to each other,
"Let's build a tower that reaches to the sky.
We'll make a name for ourselves.

Then we won't be scattered
over the face of the whole earth."

But the LORD came down to see the city
and the tower the men were building.
The LORD said, "All of them
speak the same language.
Now they will be able to do anything they plan to.
Let us mix up their language.
Then they will not understand each other."

So the LORD scattered them
from there over the whole earth.
And they stopped building the city.
The LORD mixed up the language
of the whole world there.
That's why the city was named Babel.

God's Promise to Abraham

Genesis 12; 15; 17

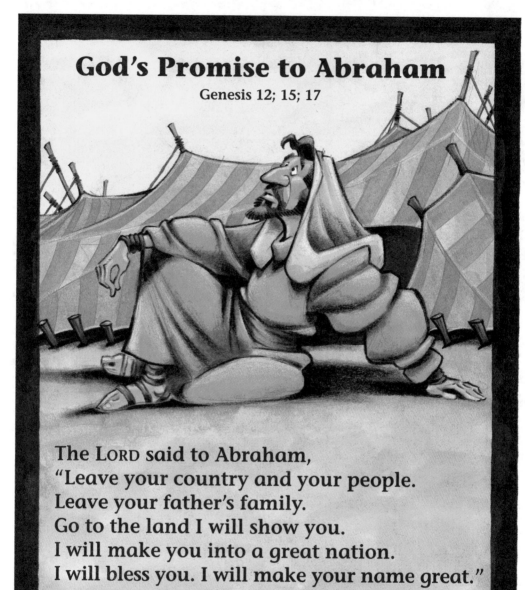

The LORD said to Abraham,
"Leave your country and your people.
Leave your father's family.
Go to the land I will show you.
I will make you into a great nation.
I will bless you. I will make your name great."

40

Abraham was 75 years old
when he left Haran.
He took his wife Sarah and his nephew Lot.
They took all the things they had.
They set out for the land of Canaan.

The LORD took Abraham outside and said,
"Look up at the sky. Count the stars.
That is how many children you will have."
When Abraham was 99 years old, the LORD
said, "Walk with me. Live without blame.

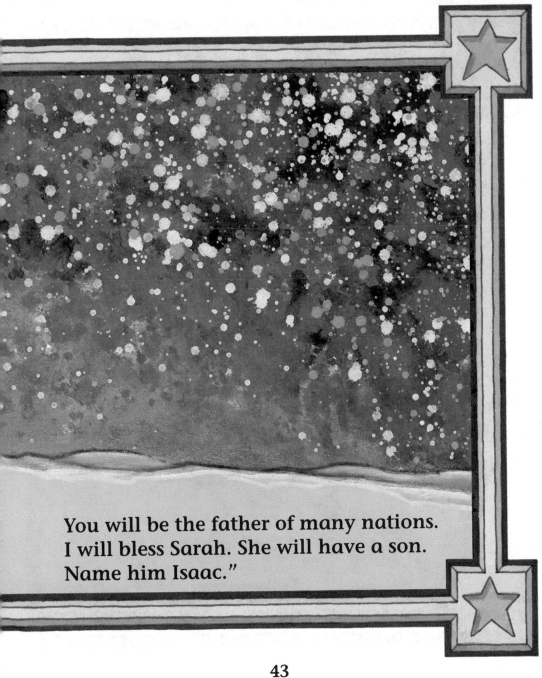

You will be the father of many nations.
I will bless Sarah. She will have a son.
Name him Isaac."

God Tests Abraham

Genesis 21 — 22

The LORD was gracious to Sarah.
He did for Sarah what he had promised to do.
Sarah had a son. Abraham named him Isaac.

Some time later God put Abraham to the test.
He said to him, "Abraham! Take your only son.
He is the one you love. Take Isaac. Go to Moriah.
Give him to me as a burnt offering."

Early the next morning Abraham got up.
He put a saddle on his donkey.
He took his son Isaac with him.
He cut enough wood for the burnt offering.
Then he started out. Abraham put the wood
for the burnt offering on his son Isaac.
He himself carried the fire and the knife.

Isaac spoke up. He said, "Father, the fire and the wood are here. But where is the lamb for the burnt offering?" Abraham answered, "God will provide the lamb, my son."

47

Abraham built an altar. He put the wood on it.
He tied up Isaac. He placed him
on top of the wood.
Then he took the knife
to kill his son.

But the angel of the LORD called out to him from
heaven, "Abraham! Do not lay a hand on the boy.
Now I know that you respect God.
You have not held back from me your only son."
Abraham looked up. There in a bush he saw a ram.
It was caught by its horns. He took the ram.
He sacrificed it instead of his son.

A Wife for Isaac

Genesis 24

Abraham said to his servant, "Go to my country and to my relatives. Get a wife for my son Isaac." The servant took ten of his master's camels and left. He made his way to the town of Nahor.

He stopped near the well outside the town.
He made the camels get down on their knees.
It was almost evening.
It was the time when women go out to get water.

Then the servant prayed, "LORD, give me success today. I will speak to a young woman.
I'll say, 'Please lower your jar so I can have a drink.'
Suppose she says, 'Have a drink of water.
I'll get some for your camels too.'
Then let her be the one you have chosen for Isaac."

Before he finished praying, Rebekah came out.
She had a jar on her shoulder.
She was very beautiful.
The servant hurried to meet her. He said,
"Please give me a little water from your jar."
After she had given him a drink, she said,
"I'll get water for your camels too."

The camels finished drinking.
Then the man took out a gold nose ring.
He also took out two gold bracelets.
He gave them to Rebekah.

Rebekah had a brother named Laban.
He hurried out to meet the man.
Laban said, "The LORD has done this."
He asked Rebekah, "Will you go
with this man?" "Yes," she said.
So the servant took Rebekah.
She became Isaac's wife,
and he loved her.

Esau and Jacob

Genesis 25

Rebekah couldn't have children.
So Isaac prayed to the LORD.
The LORD answered his prayer.
Rebekah had twin boys, Esau and Jacob.

The boys grew up. Esau became a skillful hunter.
Jacob was a quiet man.
Isaac liked the meat of wild animals.
So Esau was his favorite son.
But Rebekah's favorite was Jacob.

One day Jacob was cooking some stew.
Esau came in from the country.
He was very hungry. He said to Jacob,
"Quick! Let me have some stew!
I'm very hungry!"
Jacob replied, "First sell me the rights
that belong to you as the oldest son."
"I'm dying of hunger," Esau said.
"What good are those rights to me?"
So Esau sold Jacob all the rights that belonged to him.

Jacob gave Esau some bread and some stew.
So Esau didn't care about the rights
that belonged to him as the oldest son.

Jacob Gets the Blessing

Genesis 27

Isaac had become old.
He couldn't see anymore. He called for Esau.
Isaac said, "I'm an old man now.
Hunt some wild animals for me to eat.
Then I'll give you my blessing before I die."

Rebekah was listening.

Esau left. Then Rebekah said to Jacob,
"Listen carefully. Do what I tell you.
Bring me two young goats.
I will prepare tasty food for your father.
I want you to take it to your father to eat.
Then he'll give you his blessing before he dies."

Jacob said to his mother,
"Esau's body is covered with hair.
But my skin is smooth.
What if my father touches me?"
His mother said, "Just do what I say."
She took the best of Esau's clothes and
put them on Jacob. She covered his hands
and his neck with skins of the goats.

Then she handed Jacob the tasty food and the bread she had made. He went to his father. Jacob said, "I'm your oldest son Esau. Eat some of my wild meat." Jacob went close to his father. Isaac touched him and said,
"The voice is the voice of Jacob.
But the hands are the hands of Esau."

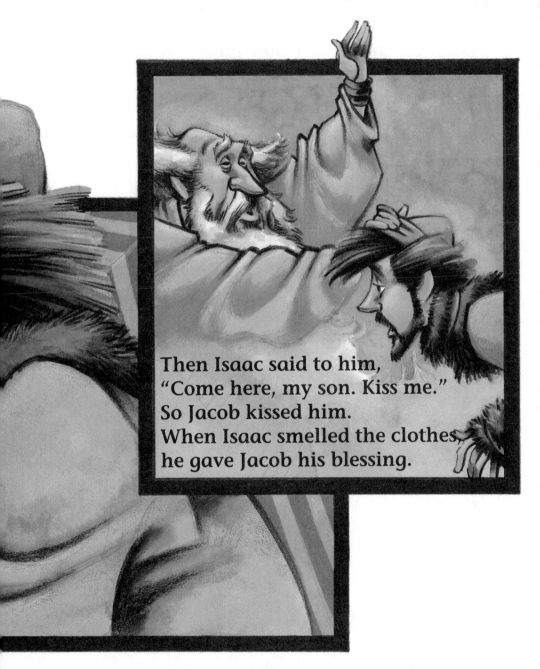

Then Isaac said to him,
"Come here, my son. Kiss me."
So Jacob kissed him.
When Isaac smelled the clothes,
he gave Jacob his blessing.

Esau was angry. He was angry because of the blessing his father had given to Jacob.

Jacob's Dream

Genesis 28

Isaac sent Jacob to get a wife.
He stopped for the night. The sun had already set.
He took one of the stones there and placed it
under his head. Then he lay down to sleep.

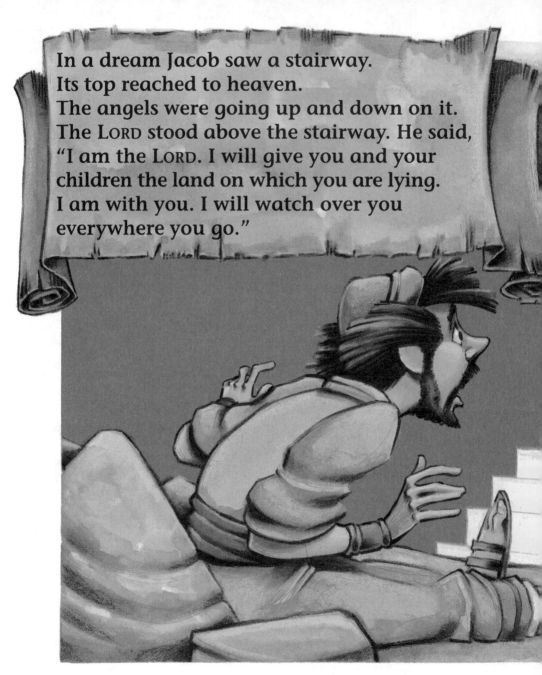

In a dream Jacob saw a stairway.
Its top reached to heaven.
The angels were going up and down on it.
The LORD stood above the stairway. He said,
"I am the LORD. I will give you and your
children the land on which you are lying.
I am with you. I will watch over you
everywhere you go."

Jacob Gets Married

Genesis 29 — 30

Laban was the brother of Jacob's mother.
Laban had two daughters, Leah and Rachel.

Jacob was in love with Rachel. He said to Laban, "I'll work for you for seven years to get your younger daughter Rachel." Laban said, "I'll give her to you." So Jacob worked for seven years to get Rachel. But they seemed like only a few days to him because he loved her so much.

Laban had a big dinner prepared.
But when evening came,
he gave his daughter Leah to Jacob.
When Jacob woke up the next morning,
there was Leah! He said to Laban,
"What have you done?
Why did you trick me?"

Laban replied, "It isn't our practice to give the younger daughter to be married before the older one. I'll give you the younger one also. But you will have to work for another seven years." So Jacob did it. He loved Rachel more than he loved Leah.

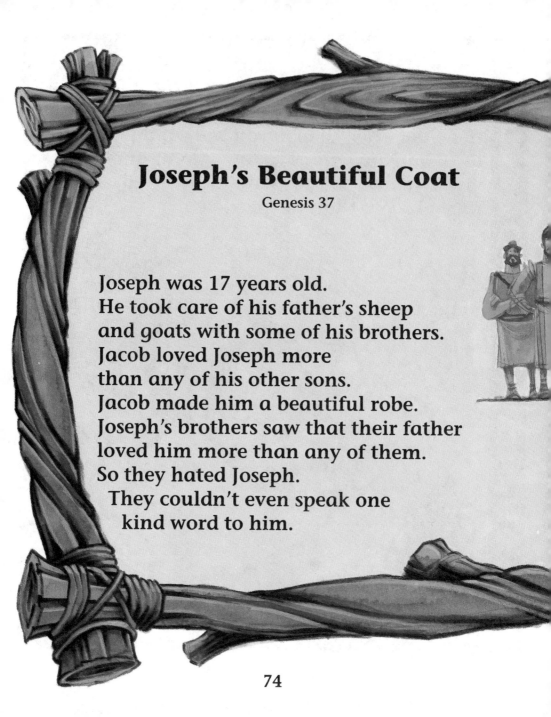

Joseph's Beautiful Coat

Genesis 37

Joseph was 17 years old.
He took care of his father's sheep
and goats with some of his brothers.
Jacob loved Joseph more
than any of his other sons.
Jacob made him a beautiful robe.
Joseph's brothers saw that their father
loved him more than any of them.
So they hated Joseph.
  They couldn't even speak one
    kind word to him.

Joseph's Dreams

Genesis 37

Joseph had a dream. He told it to his brothers.
He said, "Listen to the dream I had.
We were tying up grain in the field.
Suddenly my bundle stood up straight.
Your bundles bowed down to it."
His brothers said, "Do you plan to be our king?
Will you really rule over us?"
So they hated him because of his dream.

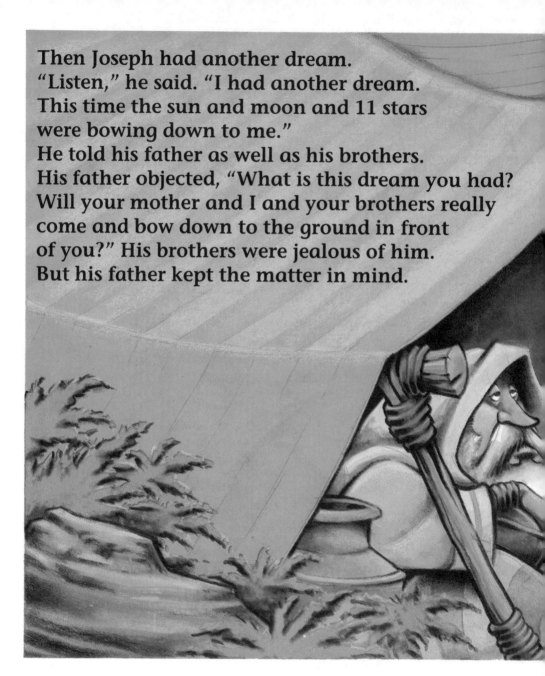

Then Joseph had another dream.
"Listen," he said. "I had another dream.
This time the sun and moon and 11 stars
were bowing down to me."
He told his father as well as his brothers.
His father objected, "What is this dream you had?
Will your mother and I and your brothers really
come and bow down to the ground in front
of you?" His brothers were jealous of him.
But his father kept the matter in mind.

The Brothers Sell Joseph

Genesis 37

Joseph's brothers had gone to take care of
their father's flocks near Shechem.
Jacob said to Joseph, "Go to your brothers.
See how they are doing. See how the flocks are."
So Joseph went to look for his brothers.

But they saw him a long way off.
Before he reached them, they made plans to kill him.
"Here comes that dreamer!" they said.
"Let's kill him.
Let's say that a wild animal ate him up."

Reuben heard them. He tried to save Joseph.
"Let's not take his life," he said.
"Throw him into this empty well."
When Joseph came to his brothers,
he was wearing his beautiful robe.
They took it away from him. And they
threw him into the well. Judah said
to his brothers, "Let's sell him. Let's not
harm him. After all, he's our brother."

83

Some traders came by.
Joseph's brothers sold him to the traders.
The traders took him to Egypt.
Then the brothers got Joseph's beautiful robe.
They killed a goat and dipped the robe in the blood.

They took it back to their father.
They said, "We found this. Take a look at it."
Jacob recognized it. He said, "It's my son's robe!
A wild animal has eaten him up."
Jacob sobbed over his son for many days.

But the traders sold Joseph
to Potiphar in Egypt.

Joseph's Brothers Go to Egypt

Genesis 42; 45; 47

People were very hungry all over the world.
Jacob found out that there was grain in Egypt.
He said to his sons, "There's grain in Egypt.
Go there. Buy some. Then we'll live and not die."
So ten of Joseph's brothers went to Egypt.

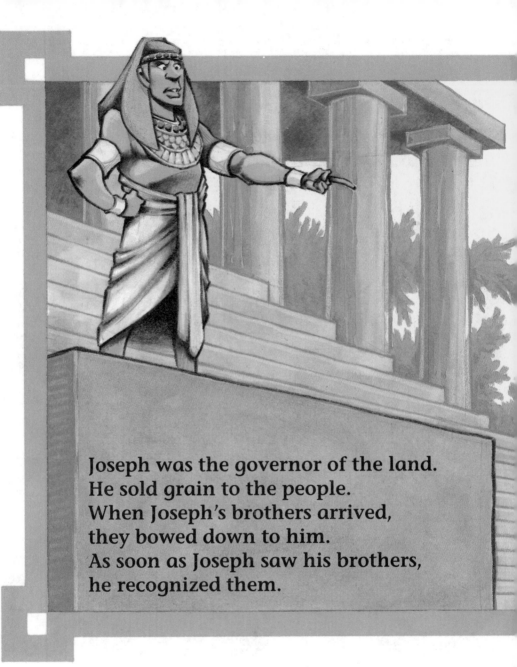

Joseph was the governor of the land.
He sold grain to the people.
When Joseph's brothers arrived,
they bowed down to him.
As soon as Joseph saw his brothers,
he recognized them.

But he pretended to be a stranger.
He spoke to them in a mean way.
He said to them, "You are spies!"
"No!" they answered.
"We've come to buy food.
We're honest men. We aren't spies."

Joseph couldn't control himself anymore. He cried out, "I am Joseph! Is my father still alive?" But his brothers weren't able to answer him. They were too afraid of him.
Joseph said to his brothers,
"Come close to me. I am your brother Joseph. I'm the one you sold into Egypt. Don't be angry with yourselves because you sold me here. God sent me ahead of you to save many lives."

So Joseph settled his father and his brothers in Egypt. He gave them property in the best part of the land.

Slaves for Pharaoh

Exodus 1

Joseph and all of his brothers died.
But the people of Israel had many children.

A new king came to power in Egypt.
"Look," he said to his people.
"The Israelites are far too many for us.
If war breaks out, they'll join our enemies.
They'll fight against us."

So the Egyptians put slave drivers over the people of Israel. They made them work hard. Then Pharaoh gave an order. He said, "Throw every baby boy into the Nile River. But let every baby girl live."

Moses Is Born

Exodus 2

A woman from the tribe of Levi had a son.
She saw that her baby was a fine child.
So she hid him for three months.

When she couldn't hide him any longer,
she got a basket. Then she placed the child in it.
She put the basket in the tall grass that grew
along the bank of the Nile River.
Miriam, the child's sister, wanted to see
what would happen to him.

Pharaoh's daughter went down
to the Nile River to take a bath.
She saw the basket in the tall grass.
She sent her slave to get it.
When she opened it, she saw the baby.
He was crying. She felt sorry for him.
"This is one of the Hebrew babies," she said.

Miriam asked Pharaoh's daughter,
"Do you want me to go and get one of the
Hebrew women? She could nurse the baby for you."
"Yes. Go," she answered.
So the girl went and got the baby's mother.

So the woman took the baby and nursed him.
When the child grew older,
she took him to Pharaoh's daughter.
He became her son. She named him Moses.

The Burning Bush

Exodus 3 — 4

Moses was taking care of the flock.
Moses saw that a bush was on fire.
But it didn't burn up.

God spoke to Moses from inside the bush.
He called out, "Moses! Moses!"
"Here I am," Moses said.
"Do not come any closer," God said.
"Take off your sandals. The place
you are standing on is holy ground."

The LORD said, "I have seen my people in Egypt.
I have heard them cry.
I am concerned about their suffering.
I have come down to save them from the Egyptians.
Now, go. I am sending you to Pharaoh.
Bring the Israelites out of Egypt."

The First Five Plagues

Exodus 5 — 9

Moses and his brother Aaron went to Pharaoh.
They said, "The LORD says, 'Let my people go
to hold a feast in my honor in the desert.' "
Pharaoh said, "Who is the LORD?
Why should I obey him? I won't let Israel go."

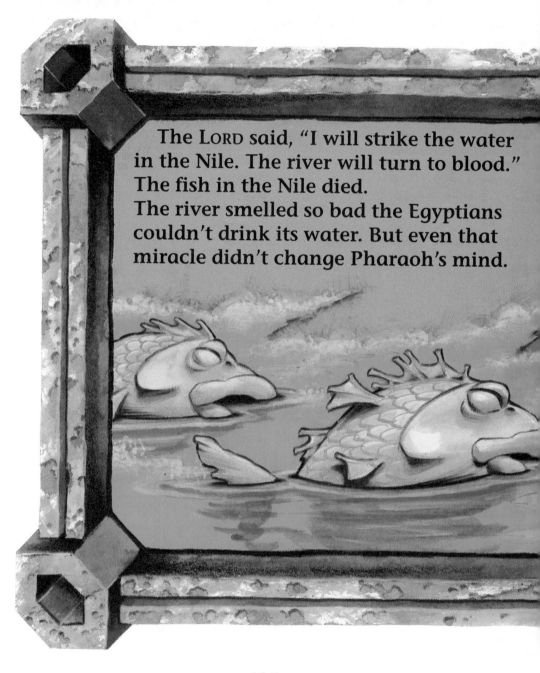

The LORD said, "I will strike the water in the Nile. The river will turn to blood." The fish in the Nile died.
The river smelled so bad the Egyptians couldn't drink its water. But even that miracle didn't change Pharaoh's mind.

107

Then the LORD said, "Let my people go."
But Pharaoh's heart became stubborn.
So the LORD said, "The Nile will be
full of frogs. They will come into
your palace and on your bed."

Pharaoh sent for Moses. He said, "Pray to the LORD to take the frogs away. Then I'll let your people go." Moses replied, "It will happen just as you say." The frogs died. But Pharaoh's heart was stubborn. He wouldn't let the people go.

Then the LORD spoke to Moses. He said, "Tell Aaron, 'Reach your wooden staff out. Strike the ground.' All over the land of Egypt the dust will turn into gnats." So they did it. The dust turned into gnats. They landed on people and animals. But Pharaoh's heart was stubborn. He wouldn't listen.

So the LORD sent large numbers of flies.
Flies poured into Pharaoh's palace.
The flies destroyed the land.
Pharaoh sent for Moses and Aaron.
Moses said, "Tomorrow the flies
will leave you. Let the people go."
But Pharaoh's heart become stubborn
that time also. He wouldn't let the people go.

Then the LORD spoke, "Let my people go. If you refuse, I will strike your horses, donkeys, camels, cattle, sheep and goats."

But Pharaoh wouldn't let the people go. So the next day all of the livestock of the Egyptians died.

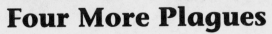

Four More Plagues

Exodus 9 — 12

The LORD said to Moses,
"Toss ashes into the air.
The ashes will turn into fine dust.
Then boils will break out
on people and animals."
But Pharaoh wouldn't listen.

Then the LORD sent thunder and hail.
Hail beat down everything that was growing.
It tore the leaves off the trees.
Pharaoh sent for Moses. "I've sinned," he said.
"Pray to the LORD. We've had enough hail."
Moses prayed. The thunder and hail stopped.
But Pharaoh sinned again.
He wouldn't let the people go.

Then the LORD made a wind blow. The wind brought locusts. The locusts covered the land and ate up everything that was left after the hail. Pharaoh sent for Moses. He said,
"Pray to the LORD to take this plague away."
Moses prayed. The LORD changed the wind.
The wind blew the locusts into the Red Sea.
But Pharaoh wouldn't let the people go.

Moses reached out his hand toward the sky.
Darkness covered Egypt for three days.
No one could see anyone else.
Pharaoh sent for Moses. He said, "Go. Worship
the LORD. Just leave your flocks and herds behind."
Moses said, "Our animals must go with us."
But Pharaoh wouldn't let the people go.
The LORD said to Moses, "I will bring one more
plague on Pharaoh. After that, he will let you go."

The Tenth Plague

Exodus 12

Moses sent for the elders of Israel.
He said, "Each man must get
a lamb for each family.
The animals must be a year old.

117

Kill the lambs when the sun goes down. Take some of the blood. Put it on the doorframes of the houses. The LORD will pass through the land to strike the Egyptians down. He'll see the blood on the doorframe. He will pass over that house. He won't let the destroying angel kill you."
The people of Israel did what the LORD commanded.

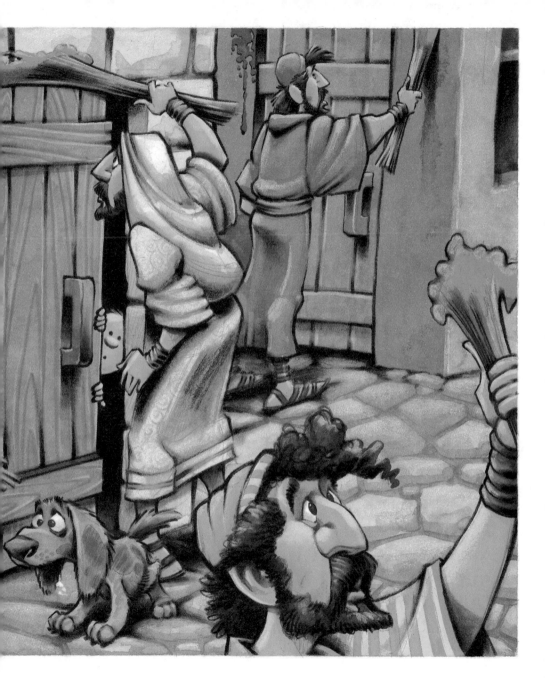

At midnight the LORD struck down every oldest
son in Egypt. There was loud crying because
someone had died in every home.
During the night, Pharaoh sent for Moses.
He said, "Get out of here! Leave my people.
Take your flocks and herds. Go."

Leaving Egypt

Exodus 12 — 13

The Egyptians begged the people to hurry.
"If you don't," they said, "we'll all die!"
The Israelites went out of Egypt.
There were about 600,000 men.
The women and children went with them.
By day the LORD went ahead of them in a pillar
of cloud. At night he led them with a pillar of fire.
They could travel by day or night.

The Red Sea

Exodus 14

Then Pharaoh and his officials changed
their minds about the people of Israel.
The Egyptians went after the Israelites.
All of Pharaoh's horses and chariots
and horsemen and troops went after them.

As Pharaoh approached, the Israelites looked up.
There were the Egyptians!
The Israelites were terrified.
They said to Moses, "What have you done?
It would have been better to serve
the Egyptians than to die in the desert!"
Moses answered the people, "Don't be afraid.
The LORD will fight for you."

Then Moses reached his hand
out over the Red Sea.
All that night the LORD
pushed the sea back.
He turned the sea into dry land.

The people went through the sea on
dry ground. There was a wall of water
on their right and on their left.

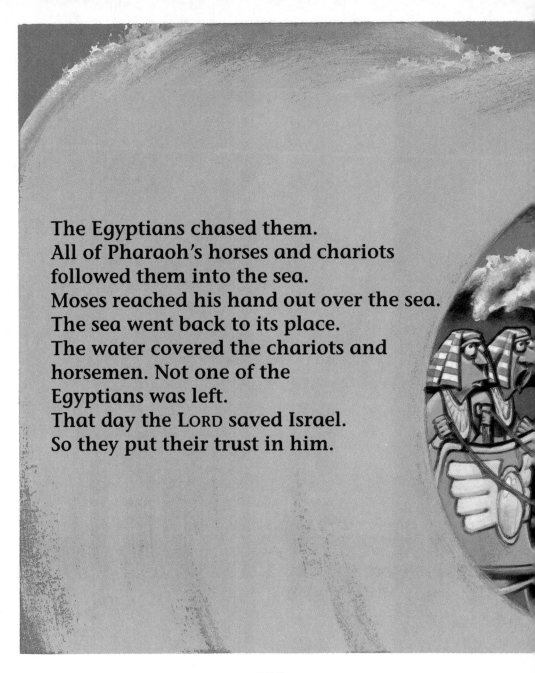

The Egyptians chased them.
All of Pharaoh's horses and chariots
followed them into the sea.
Moses reached his hand out over the sea.
The sea went back to its place.
The water covered the chariots and
horsemen. Not one of the
Egyptians was left.
That day the LORD saved Israel.
So they put their trust in him.

Manna and Quail

Exodus 16

The whole community told Moses they weren't happy. "In Egypt we ate all the food we wanted. But you have brought us out into this desert to die of hunger."

The LORD said, "I have heard the people talking about how unhappy they are. Tell them, 'When the sun goes down, you will eat meat. In the morning you will be filled with bread.'" That evening quail came and covered the camp.

In the morning thin flakes appeared on the desert floor. Moses said, "It's the bread the LORD has given you to eat." The people called the bread manna. They ate manna for 40 years until they reached the border of Canaan.

Moses at Mount Sinai

Exodus 19 — 20

Three months after the Israelites left Egypt,
they came to the Desert of Sinai. They camped
in the desert in front of the mountain.

There was thunder and lightning.
A thick cloud covered the mountain.
A trumpet gave a very loud blast.
Everyone in the camp trembled.

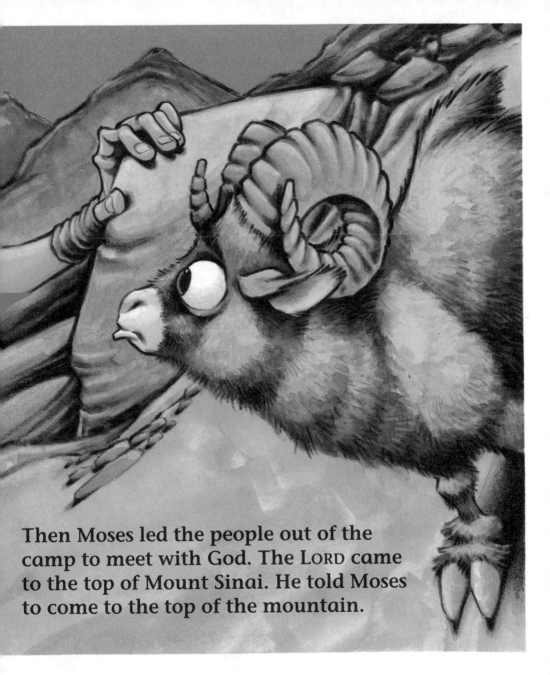

Then Moses led the people out of the camp to meet with God. The LORD came to the top of Mount Sinai. He told Moses to come to the top of the mountain.

Here are all of the words God spoke.

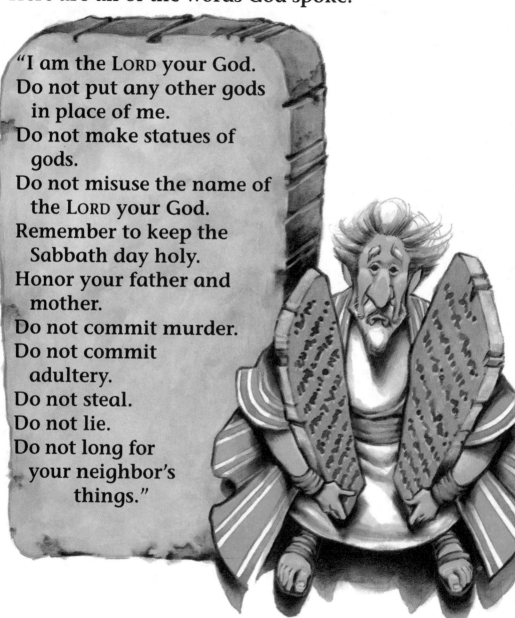

"I am the LORD your God.
Do not put any other gods
   in place of me.
Do not make statues of
   gods.
Do not misuse the name of
   the LORD your God.
Remember to keep the
   Sabbath day holy.
Honor your father and
   mother.
Do not commit murder.
Do not commit
   adultery.
Do not steal.
Do not lie.
Do not long for
   your neighbor's
         things."

The Calf of Gold

Exodus 24; 32 — 34

Moses stayed on the mountain for 40 days and 40 nights. The people gathered around Aaron. They said to him, "Make us a god that will lead us. We don't know what has happened to Moses."

All of the people took off their earrings. They brought them to Aaron. He made them into a statue of a god. It looked like a calf. Then the people said, "Israel, here is your god."
So they sat down to eat and drink. They got up to dance wildly in front of their god.

The LORD spoke to Moses, "Go! Your people have made a statue that looks like a calf."

Moses went down the mountain.
He had the two tablets in his hand.
The tablets were the work of God.
As Moses approached the camp, he saw
the calf. He burned with anger.

He threw the tablets out of his hands.
They broke into pieces. He took the calf the
people had made. He burned it in the fire.
Moses said to the people, "You have
committed a terrible sin. I will go to the LORD.
If I pray, he will forgive your sin."

Water Out of the Rock

Exodus 17

The Israelites camped,
but there wasn't any water to drink.
They argued with Moses.
They said, "Give us water to drink.
Did you want us to die of thirst?"
Moses cried out to the LORD,
"What am I to do with these people?
They are almost ready to kill me."

The LORD answered,
"Walk ahead of the people.
I will stand in front of you by the
rock at Mount Horeb. Hit the rock.
Water will come out of it
for the people to drink."
So Moses hit the rock.

141

The Bronze Snake

Numbers 21

The people of Israel grew tired.
So they spoke against God.
"Why have you brought us out of Egypt
to die in the desert? We don't have bread!
We don't have water! We hate this awful food!"
The LORD sent poisonous snakes among the people.
The snakes bit them. Many people died.
The others said, "We sinned.
Pray that the LORD will take the snakes away."
So Moses prayed for the people.
The LORD said to Moses, "Make a snake.
Put it on a pole. Anyone who is bitten
can look at it and remain alive."

So Moses made a bronze snake on a pole.
Anyone who was bitten and looked
at the bronze snake remained alive.

Exploring Canaan

Numbers 13 — 14

Moses sent some men to check out the land of
Canaan. He said, "See what the land is like.
See whether the people are strong or weak.
What kind of towns do they live in?
How is the soil? Are there trees on it?"

The men went and checked out the land.
They cut off a branch that had grapes on it.
Two of them carried it on a pole between them.
At the end of 40 days, the men returned.

The men reported to Moses and Aaron.
They said, "It really does have plenty of
milk and honey! But the people are powerful.
Their cities are very large.
We can't attack those people.
They are stronger than we are."

Joshua and Caleb were two of the men who had checked out the land. They said, "The LORD is with us. Don't be afraid."

That night the people of Israel grumbled. "Why is the LORD bringing us to this land? We're going to be killed." The LORD replied, "Not all of you will enter the land. Caleb will enter it. So will Joshua. They are the only ones who will enter the land. I will bring your children in. As for you, you will die in the desert. For 40 years you will suffer."

The Fall of Jericho

Joshua 6

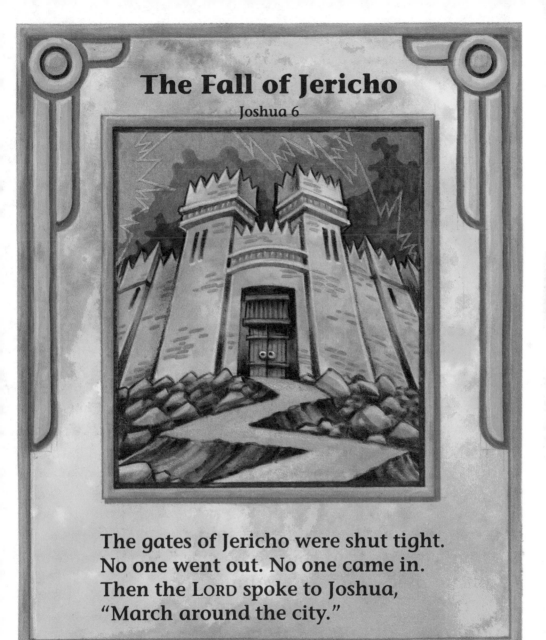

The gates of Jericho were shut tight.
No one went out. No one came in.
Then the LORD spoke to Joshua,
"March around the city."

So Joshua gave an order. He said,
"Move out! March around the city." So the
fighting men marched around the
city once. Then the men returned to
camp. They did these things for six days.

On the seventh day, they got up at sunrise.
They marched around the city seven times.
On the seventh time around, Joshua said,
"Shout! The LORD has given you the city!"
The priests blew the trumpets. The men gave
a loud shout. Then the wall fell down. Every man
charged straight in. So they took the city.

Gideon Wins the War

Judges 7

Gideon and his men camped at a spring.
The Lord spoke to Gideon,
"You have too many men.
Those who tremble with fear can turn back."
So 22,000 men left. But 10,000 remained.

The LORD spoke again,
"There are still too many men."
So Gideon took the men to the water.
Three hundred men brought the water
to their mouths with their hands.
All the rest got down on their knees to drink.
The LORD said, "With the help of the
300 men I will save you.
Let the other men go home."

Gideon put a trumpet and an empty jar into the hands of each man. He put a torch inside each jar. "Watch me," he told them. "Do what I do." Gideon and the men reached the enemy camp at night. Gideon and his men blew their trumpets. They smashed their jars. They shouted, "A sword for the LORD and for Gideon!" The enemy ran away. They were crying as they ran.

Samson and Delilah

Judges 15 — 16

Samson led Israel for 20 years.
In those days the Philistines were in the land.
Samson fell in love with Delilah.
The Philistines said to her,
"See if you can get him to tell you
the secret of why he's so strong."
So Delilah spoke to Samson.
"Tell me the secret of why you are so strong."

Samson answered, "Let someone tie me with new ropes. I'll become as weak as any man." Delilah got new ropes. She tied him up. She called, "Samson! The Philistines are attacking you!" But he snapped the ropes off his arms.

Delilah said, "You have been telling me lies.
Tell me how you can be tied up."
He replied, "Weave the seven braids
of my hair on a loom. I'll become weak."
So while Samson was sleeping, Delilah took
the seven braids of his hair. She wove them
into a loom. Again she called out,
"Samson! The Philistines are attacking you!"
He woke up. He pulled up the loom.

She continued to pester
him until he was
sick and tired of it.
So he told her everything.
"If you shave my head,
I'll be as weak as any man.

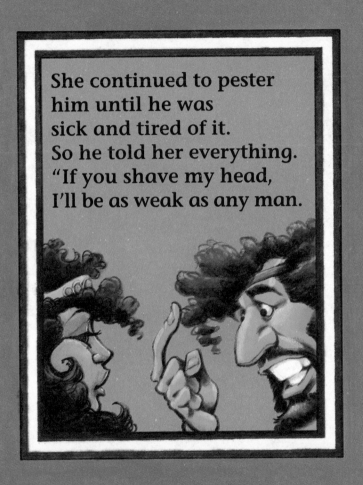

Delilah got Samson to go to sleep on her lap. She called for someone to shave off his hair. And he wasn't strong anymore.

Then the Philistines grabbed him.
They poked his eyes out. They put chains on him.
But his hair began to grow again.

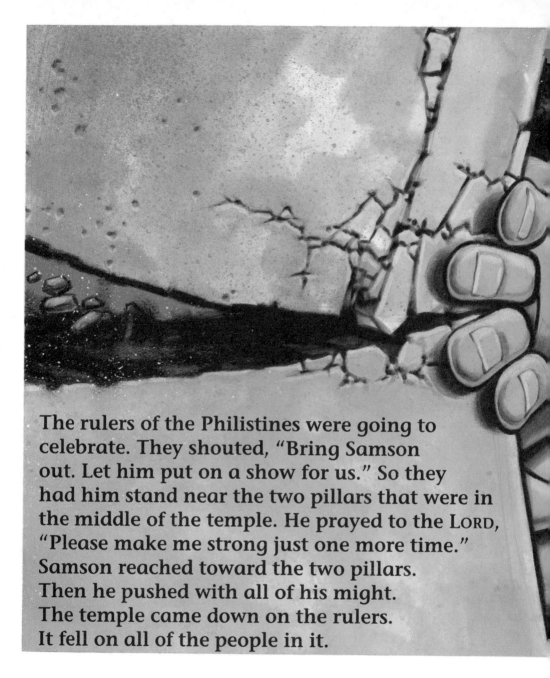

The rulers of the Philistines were going to
celebrate. They shouted, "Bring Samson
out. Let him put on a show for us." So they
had him stand near the two pillars that were in
the middle of the temple. He prayed to the LORD,
"Please make me strong just one more time."
Samson reached toward the two pillars.
Then he pushed with all of his might.
The temple came down on the rulers.
It fell on all of the people in it.

163

Naomi and Ruth

Ruth 1

There wasn't enough food in the land. A man, his wife and two sons went to live in Moab for a while.

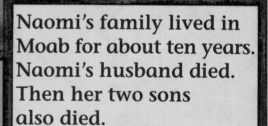

Naomi's family lived in Moab for about ten years. Naomi's husband died. Then her two sons also died.

The LORD had begun to provide food again.

On the road back to Judah, Naomi spoke to her two daughters-in-law. "Both of you go back. Find another husband."

Then Orpah kissed her mother-in-law good-by.

But Ruth held on to her. Ruth said,
"Don't try to make me leave you.
Where you go I'll go. Where you stay I'll stay.
Your people will be my people.
Your God will be my God."
So Naomi returned from Moab.
Ruth, her daughter-in-law, came with her.

JUDAH
MOAB
MT. NEBO
EDOM
BETHLEHEM

God Calls Samuel

1 Samuel 3

One night Eli the priest was lying down. He couldn't see very well. Samuel was also lying down. The LORD called out to Samuel. Samuel ran over to Eli. He said, "Here I am. You called out to me."
But Eli said, "I didn't call. Go back and lie down." So he went and lay down.

Again the LORD called out, "Samuel!"
Samuel got up and went to Eli. He said,
"Here I am. You called me."
"My son," Eli said, "I didn't call you.
Go back and lie down."
The LORD called Samuel for the third time.
Samuel got up and went to Eli. He said,
"Here I am. You called out to me."
Then Eli realized that the LORD was calling.
Eli told Samuel, "Go. Lie down.
If someone calls again, say, 'Speak, LORD.
I'm listening.'" So Samuel went and lay down.

169

The LORD called out, just as he had done the other times, "Samuel! Samuel!" Samuel replied, "Speak. I'm listening." And as Samuel grew up, the LORD was with him.

Saul Becomes King

1 Samuel 8; 10

The elders of Israel gathered together. They said to Samuel, "We want a king." So Samuel prayed to the LORD. Finally Saul was chosen. But when the people looked for him, he wasn't there. The LORD said, "He has hidden himself among the supplies."

They brought him out. When he stood up, he
was a head taller than any of them. Samuel said,
"Look at the man the LORD has chosen!
There isn't anyone like him among the people."
Then the people shouted,
"May the king live a long time!"

A New King

Samuel 16

The LORD said to Samuel,
"Fill your horn with oil. I am sending you
to Jesse in Bethlehem. I have chosen one
of his sons to be king. Anoint the one I
point out to you."

Samuel saw Eliab. He thought, "This has to be the one the LORD wants." But the LORD said to Samuel, "I have not chosen him. I do not look at the things people look at. They look at someone on the outside. But I look at what is in the heart."

Jesse had his sons walk in front of Samuel.
But Samuel said, "The LORD hasn't chosen them.
Are these the only sons you have?"
Jesse answered, "My youngest son
is taking care of the sheep."
Samuel said, "Send for him."

Jesse sent for his son David. He had a fine appearance and handsome features. Then the LORD said, "Anoint him. He is the one." From that day on, the Spirit of the LORD came on David.

David and Goliath

1 Samuel 17

The Philistines gathered their army for war. The Philistine army was camped on one hill. Israel's army was on another.

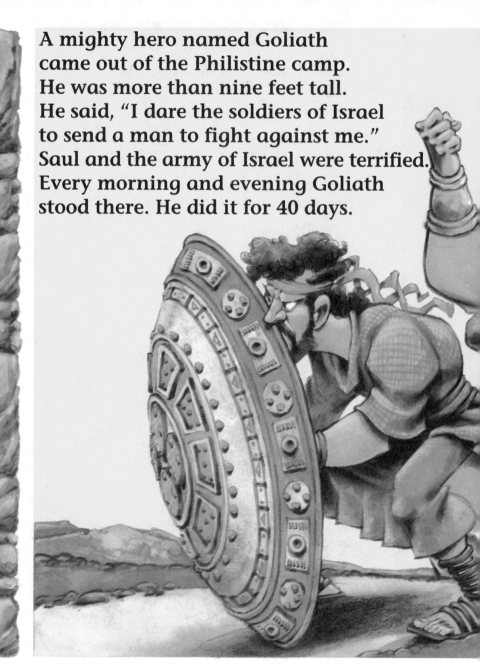

A mighty hero named Goliath
came out of the Philistine camp.
He was more than nine feet tall.
He said, "I dare the soldiers of Israel
to send a man to fight against me."
Saul and the army of Israel were terrified.
Every morning and evening Goliath
stood there. He did it for 40 days.

179

Jesse said to his son David, "Get ten loaves of bread.
Take all of it to your brothers. Hurry to their camp.
Take along these chunks of cheese.
Find out how your brothers are doing.
They are with Saul fighting against the Philistines."
Early in the morning, David left his father's
flock, loaded up the food and started out.

David ran to the battle lines and greeted his brothers. As David was talking with them, Goliath stepped forward. He again dared someone to fight him.

And David heard it.

David said to Saul, "I'll fight him."
Saul replied, "You are too young."
But David said to Saul, "The LORD saved
me from the lion. He saved me from the bear.
He'll save me from this Philistine."

Then David went to a stream and chose five smooth stones. He took his sling and approached Goliath. Goliath looked David over. He saw how young he was. And he hated him. He said, "Why are you coming at me with sticks? Do you think I'm a dog?"

David said to Goliath, "You are coming to fight me
with a sword. But I'm coming against you
in the name of the LORD who rules over all."
David ran quickly to the battle line.
He took out a stone. He put it in his sling.
He slung it at Goliath. The stone hit him on the
forehead and sank into it.
He fell to the ground on his face.
The Philistines saw that their hero was dead.
So they turned around and ran away.

Solomon Asks to Be Wise

1 Kings 1 — 3

The time came near for David to die.
David made Solomon king.
The LORD appeared to Solomon in a dream.
God said, "Ask for anything you want."
Solomon said, "LORD, you have made me king.
But I don't know how to carry out my duties.
Give me a heart that understands."
The LORD was pleased and said,
"I will give you a wise heart.
And I will give you what you have not asked for.
I will give you riches and honor."

Solomon Judges Wisely

1 Kings 3

Two women came to Solomon.
One of them said,
"This woman and I live in the same house.
I had a baby.
Three days after my child was born,
this woman also had a baby.
During the night this woman's baby died.
She took my son while I was asleep.

The next morning, I got up to nurse my son.
But he was dead! I looked at him closely.
And I saw that it wasn't my baby."
The other woman said, "No!
The living baby is my son.
The dead one belongs to you."
So they argued in front of the king.

The king said,
"Bring me a sword.
Cut the living child in
two. Give half to one
woman and half
to the other."
The woman whose
son was alive was
filled with concern.
She said, "Please give
her the baby!
Don't kill him!"
But the other woman
said, "Neither one of
us will have him.
Cut him in two!"
Then the king
made his decision.
"Give the baby to
the first woman.
Don't kill him.
She's his mother."
All of Israel heard
about the king's
decision. They saw
that God had
given him wisdom.

Solomon Builds the Temple

1 Kings 6

Solomon began to build the temple of the LORD.
All the stones for building the temple were shaped
where they were cut. So hammers, chisels and
iron tools couldn't be heard where the temple
was being built. The inside of the temple
was covered with cedar wood. Gourds and
open flowers were carved on the wood.
Solomon covered the inside of the temple with gold.
He covered the altar with gold.
On the walls around the temple he carved
cherubim, palm trees and open flowers.
So Solomon built the temple and finished it.
Solomon had spent seven years building it.

Elijah Is Fed by Ravens

1 Kings 16 — 17

Ahab became king of Israel. He did more
evil things than any of the kings before
him. Elijah the prophet said to Ahab,
"I serve the LORD.
There won't be any dew or rain
on the land during the next few years."
Then a message from the LORD
came to Elijah.
"Go and hide in the Kerith Valley.
You will drink water from the brook.
I have ordered some ravens to feed you."
So Elijah went to the Kerith Valley.
The ravens brought him bread and meat
in the morning and in the evening.
He drank water from the brook.

Elijah Visits a Widow

1 Kings 17

Some time later the brook dried up. A message came to Elijah from the LORD, "Go to Zarephath. I have commanded a widow to supply you with food."

So Elijah went to Zarephath.
He came to the town gate.
A widow was there gathering sticks.

Elijah called out to her, "Would you bring me a little water? Bring me bread too."

"I don't have any bread," she replied, "Only a handful of flour and a little oil. I am gathering a few sticks to take home. I'll make one last meal for myself and my son. We'll eat it. After that, we'll die."

Elijah said, "Don't be afraid. Go home. Do what you have said. But first make a little bread for me. Make it out of what you have. Then make some for yourself and your son. The flour will not be used up. The jug will always have oil in it. You will have flour and oil until the day the LORD sends rain on the land."

She went away and did what Elijah told her.

199

So Elijah had food every day.
There was also food for the
woman and her family.

Elijah on Mount Carmel

1 Kings 18

Ahab went to where Elijah was.
Elijah said, "You have turned
away from the LORD.
Now send for people from all over Israel.
Tell them to meet me on Mount Carmel.
Bring the 450 prophets of Baal."

So Ahab gathered the prophets. Elijah said,
"If the LORD is the one and only God, follow him.
But if Baal is the one and only God, serve him.
Get two bulls. Let Baal's prophets put one
on the wood. But don't set fire to it.

I'll put the other bull on the wood.
But I won't set fire to it. You pray to your god.
I'll pray to the LORD. The god who sends fire
is the one and only God."

The 450 prophets of Baal prayed
to Baal from morning until noon.
"Baal! Answer us!" they shouted.
But no one answered.

At noon Elijah began to tease them.
"Shout louder!" he said. "Maybe he's sleeping."

So they shouted louder. They cut themselves with swords until their blood flowed. They continued with all their might until evening.
But there wasn't any reply.

Then Elijah said to the people, "Come here."
He rebuilt the altar of the LORD.
He dug a ditch around it. Then he said,
"Fill four large jars with water. Pour it on
the offering and the wood. Do it three times."
So they did. The water ran down
around the altar. It even filled the ditch.

Elijah stepped forward. "Lord, answer me.
Then these people will know you are the one
and only God." The fire of the Lord came.
It burned up the sacrifice, the wood, the
stones, the soil and all the water.
The people saw it. They cried out,
"The Lord is the one and only God!"

Elijah Goes to Heaven

1 Kings 19; 2 Kings 2

Elisha became Elijah's assistant.
They were walking along and talking together.
Suddenly a chariot and horses appeared. Fire
was all around them. The chariot came between
the two men. Then Elijah went up to heaven
in a strong wind. And Elisha didn't see Elijah
anymore. The prophets were watching. They said,
"The spirit of Elijah has been given to Elisha."

Naaman's Skin Disease

2 Kings 5

Naaman was commander
of the army of Aram.
He was a brave soldier.
But he had a skin disease.

A young girl from Israel
became a servant of Naaman's wife.
She said to the woman, "I wish
my master would see the prophet.
He would heal my master of his skin disease."

Naaman went to the king. He told him what
the girl said. "You should go," the king replied.

So Naaman went to see Elisha.
Elisha sent a messenger out to him.
"Go. Wash yourself in the Jordan River
seven times. Then your skin will be healed."

But Naaman said, "I thought he would pray to the LORD. I thought he would wave his hand over my skin. Then I would be healed." So he went away burning with anger.

Naaman's servants said, "What if Elisha had told you to do some great thing? Wouldn't you have done it? But he only said, 'Wash yourself.' You should be even more willing to do that!"

So Naaman went to the Jordan.
He dipped himself in it seven times. His skin became clean like the skin of a young boy.

Naaman went and stood in front of Elisha.
He said, "Now I know that there is no
God in the whole world except in Israel."

Joash Repairs the Temple

2 Chronicles 24

Joash was seven years old when he became king.
He ruled in Jerusalem for 40 years.
Joash did what was right in the eyes of the Lord.
Joash decided to make the temple
look like new again.
Joash commanded that a wooden chest be made.
It was placed near the temple.
All of the people gladly brought their money.
They dropped it into the chest until it was full.

The king gave it to the men who were doing the work on the temple. They hired people to repair the temple. The men who were in charge of the work did their best. They rebuilt God's temple.

The Shepherd's Psalm

Psalm 23

The Lᴏᴀᴀ is my shepherd. He gives me
   everything I need.
  He lets me lie down in fields of green grass.
He leads me beside quiet waters.
  He gives me new strength.
He guides me in the right paths
  for the honor of his name.
Even though I walk
  through the darkest valley,
I will not be afraid.
  You are with me.
Your shepherd's rod and staff
  comfort me.

You prepare a feast for me
   right in front of my enemies.
You pour oil on my head.
   My cup runs over.
Your goodness and love will follow me
   all the days of my life.
And I will live in the house of the LORD
   forever.

A Psalm for Giving Thanks

Psalm 100

Shout to the LORD with joy, everyone on earth.
   Worship the LORD with gladness.
   Come to him with songs of joy.
I want you to realize that the LORD is God.
   He made us, and we belong to him.
We are his people.
   We are the sheep belonging to his flock.
Give thanks as you enter the gates of his temple.
   Give praise as you enter its courtyards.
   Give thanks to him and praise his name.
The LORD is good. His faithful love continues forever.
   It will last for all time to come.

A Praise Psalm

Psalm 150

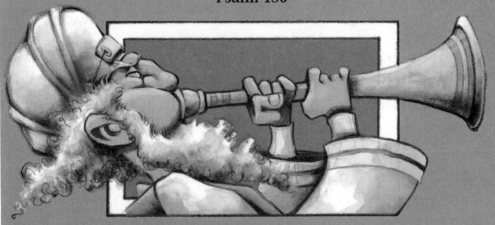

Praise the LORD.
Praise God in his holy temple.
    Praise him in his mighty heavens.
Praise him for his powerful acts.
    Praise him because he is greater than anything
    else.
Praise him by blowing trumpets.
    Praise him with harps and lyres.
Praise him with tambourines and dancing.
    Praise him with stringed instruments and flutes.
Praise him with clashing cymbals.
    Praise him with clanging cymbals.
Let everything that has breath praise the LORD.
Praise the LORD.

A Time for Everything

Ecclesiastes 3

There is a time for everything.
There's a time for everything done on earth.
There is a time to be born. And a time to die.
A time to plant. And a time to pull up.
There is a time to kill. And a time to heal.
There is a time to tear down. And a time to build.
There is a time to cry. And a time to laugh.
There is a time to be sad. And a time to dance.
A time to scatter stones. And a time to gather them.
A time to hug. And a time not to.
A time to search. And a time to stop.
A time to keep.
   And a time to throw
      away.
A time to tear.
   And a time to mend.
A time to be silent.
   And a time to speak.
A time to love.
   And a time to hate.
A time for war.
   And a time for peace.

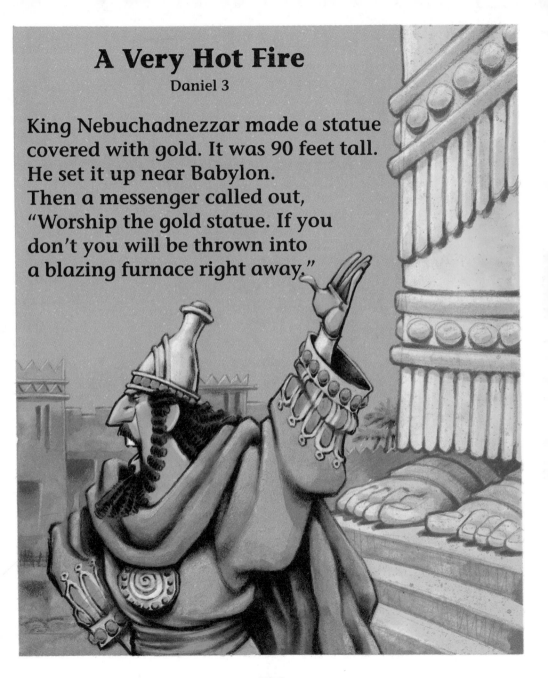

A Very Hot Fire

Daniel 3

King Nebuchadnezzar made a statue covered with gold. It was 90 feet tall. He set it up near Babylon. Then a messenger called out, "Worship the gold statue. If you don't you will be thrown into a blazing furnace right away."

Some men said, "Shadrach, Meshach
and Abednego don't pay any attention.
They refuse to worship the statue."

Nebuchadnezzar burned with anger.
The king said, "Shadrach, Meshach and
Abednego, worship the statue I made.
If you don't you will be thrown
into a blazing furnace.
Then what god will be able to save you?"
They replied, "The God we serve is able to
bring us out of it alive. But even if
our God wouldn't save us,
we still wouldn't worship
the gold statue."

Then Nebuchadnezzar ordered the furnace
heated seven times hotter than usual.
He told his men to throw Shadrach, Meshach
and Abednego into the blazing furnace.
The furnace was so hot that its
flames killed the soldiers who
threw them into it.

The three men were firmly tied up.
And they fell into the blazing fire.
Then Nebuchadnezzar leaped to his feet.
"Look! I see four men walking around in the fire.
The fourth man looks like a son of the gods."

Then the king shouted, "Shadrach, Meshach
and Abednego, come out!"
So they came out of the fire.
The fire hadn't harmed their bodies.
Not one hair on their heads was burned.
Their robes weren't burned either.
And they didn't even smell like smoke.

Then Nebuchadnezzar said,
"May the God of Shadrach, Meshach and Abednego
be praised! No other god can save people that way."

Words on the Wall

Daniel 5

King Belshazzar gave a big dinner.
He gave orders to his servants to bring in some
gold and silver cups. They were cups his father
had taken from the temple in Jerusalem.
The king and his nobles drank from them.
As they drank the wine, they praised their gods.

Suddenly the fingers of a human hand appeared. They wrote on the wall.
The king watched the hand as it wrote. His face turned pale. He became so afraid that his knees knocked together.
All of the king's wise men couldn't read the writing. They couldn't tell him what it meant.

233

So Daniel was brought to the king.
Daniel answered the king, "Here is what those
words mean. God has limited the time of your rule.
He has brought it to an end. Your authority
over your kingdom will be taken away.
It will be given to the Medes and Persians."

Then Belshazzar dressed Daniel in purple clothes and put a gold chain around his neck.
He was made a ruler in the kingdom.
That very night Belshazzar was killed.
His kingdom was given to Darius the Mede.

Daniel and the Lions

Daniel 6

Daniel went home to his upstairs room.
Its windows opened toward Jerusalem.
He went to his room three times a day to pray.
He got down on his knees
and gave thanks to God.

Some men saw him praying.
They said to the king, "Didn't you sign an order? For the next 30 days none of your people could pray to any god except you. If they did, they would be thrown into the lions' den." The king answered, "The order must be obeyed."
The men spoke again, "Daniel doesn't obey the order. He still prays to his God."

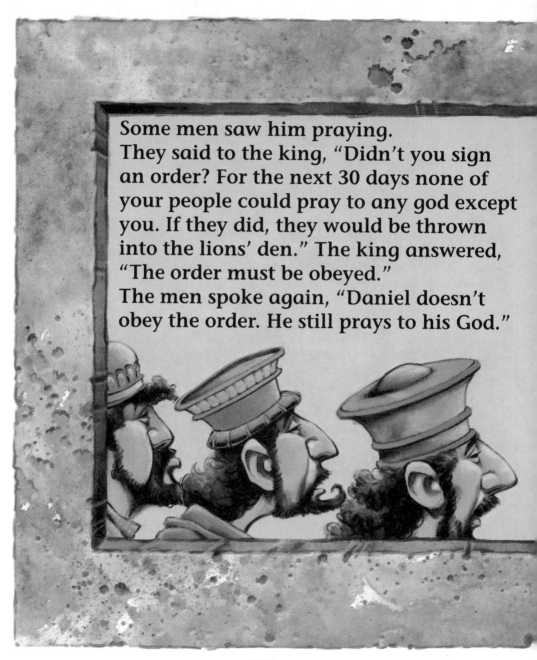

So the king gave the order. Daniel was
brought out and thrown into the lions' den.
The king said to him,
"May God save you."

The king returned to his palace.
He didn't eat anything that night.
He couldn't sleep.
As soon as the sun began to rise,
the king got up.
He hurried to the lions' den.

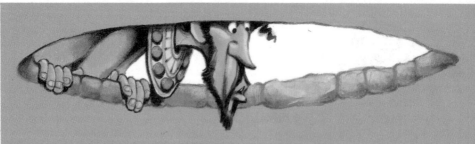

When he got near it, he called out to Daniel,
"Daniel! You serve the living God.
Has he been able to save you from the lions?"

Daniel answered, "My God sent his angel. And his angel shut the mouths of the lions. They haven't hurt me at all."
The king was filled with joy. He ordered his servants to lift Daniel out of the den.

Jonah and the Huge Fish

Jonah 1 — 2

The LORD said, "Go to the great city of Nineveh. Preach against it." But Jonah ran away from the LORD. He sailed for Tarshish.

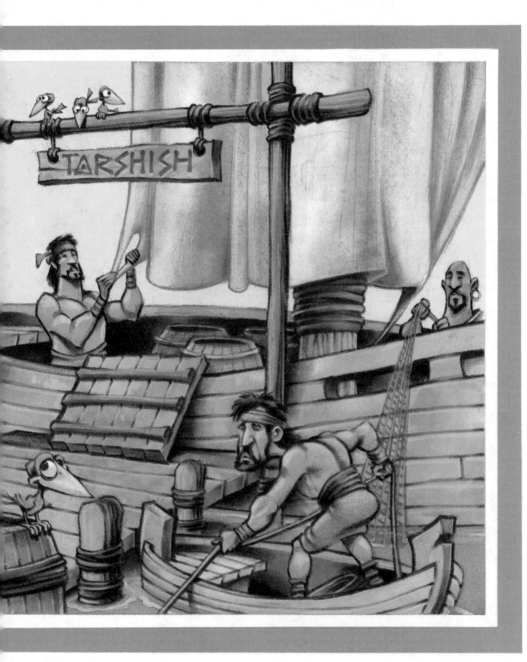

The LORD sent a wild storm.
The ship was in danger of breaking apart.
The sailors were afraid.
Each cried out to his own god.

But Jonah had gone below deck.
He lay down and fell into a deep sleep.
The captain went to him and said,
"How can you sleep? Get up.
Call to your god for help."

The sea was getting rougher.
So the sailors asked Jonah,
"What should we do to make the sea calm down?"
"Pick me up and throw me into the sea," he replied.
"Then it will become calm. It's my fault
that this terrible storm has come on you."
Instead of doing what he said, the men did their
best to row back to land. But they couldn't.
The sea got even rougher than before.

Then they threw Jonah overboard.
The stormy sea became calm.
When the men saw that, they began to
have great respect for the LORD.
But the LORD sent a huge fish to swallow Jonah.

Jonah was inside the fish for
three days and three nights.
From inside the fish Jonah prayed to the LORD.
The fish spit Jonah up onto dry land.
Jonah obeyed the LORD. He went to Nineveh.

NEW
TESTAMENT

Mary and the Angel

Luke 1

God sent the angel Gabriel to a virgin.
The girl was engaged to a man named Joseph.
The virgin's name was Mary.
The angel said, "The Lord is with you."
Mary was very upset.
But the angel said, "Do not be afraid, Mary.
God is pleased with you.
You will give birth to a son.
You must name him Jesus."

253

"How can this happen?" Mary asked.
The angel answered, "The Holy Spirit
will come to you. The holy one that is born
will be called the Son of God.
Nothing is impossible with God."

"I serve the Lord," Mary answered.
"May it happen to me just as you said it would."
Then the angel left her.

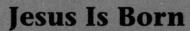

Luke 2

Caesar Augustus required that a list be made of everyone in the whole Roman world. All went to their own towns to be listed.

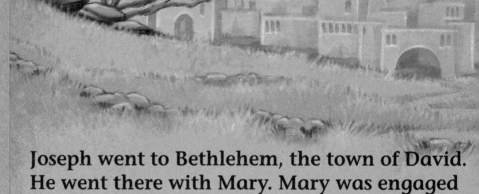

Joseph went to Bethlehem, the town of David. He went there with Mary. Mary was engaged to him. She was expecting a baby.

While Joseph and Mary were there,
the time came for the child to be born.
She gave birth to her first baby. It was a boy.
She wrapped him in large strips of cloth.
Then she placed him in a manger.
There was no room for them in the inn.

The Shepherds and the Angels

Luke 2

There were shepherds living in the fields.
It was night.
They were looking after their sheep.

An angel of the Lord appeared to them.
The glory of the Lord shone around them.
And they were terrified.

But the angel said to them, "Do not be afraid. I bring you good news of great joy. It is for all the people. Today in the town of David a Savior has been born. He is Christ the Lord. You will find a baby wrapped in strips of cloth and lying in a manger."

Suddenly a large group of angels appeared.
They were praising God. They said, "May glory
be given to God in heaven! And peace on earth."

The angels left and went into heaven.
The shepherds hurried off.

They found Mary and Joseph and the baby.
The baby was lying in the manger.

After the shepherds had seen him, they told
everyone. They reported what the angel had said.
All who heard it were amazed
at what the shepherds said.

Taking Jesus to the Temple

Luke 2

Joseph and Mary took Jesus to Jerusalem.
They presented him to the Lord.
In Jerusalem there was a man named Simeon.
The Holy Spirit had told Simeon that he would
not die before he had seen the Lord's Christ.
The Spirit led him into the temple courtyard.
Then Jesus' parents brought the child in.
Simeon took Jesus in his arms and praised God.

There was also a prophet named Anna.
Anna was very old.
She never left the temple.
She worshiped night and day.
Anna came up to Jesus' family.
She gave thanks to God.

Joseph and Mary
returned to their own
town. And Jesus grew
and became strong.
He was very wise.
He was blessed
by God's grace.

The Wise Men Visit Jesus
Matthew 2

After Jesus' birth, Wise Men
from the east came to Jerusalem.
They asked,
"Where is the child who has been
born to be king of the Jews?
When we were in the east,
we saw his star.
Now we have come
to worship him."

271

King Herod heard about it. He was upset.

Herod called for the Wise Men.
He found out when the star had appeared.

He sent them to Bethlehem. He said,
"Make a careful search for the child.
As soon as you find him, bring me a report.
Then I can go and worship him too."

The Wise Men went on their way.
The star went ahead of them. It finally stopped
over the place where the child was.
When they saw the star,
they were filled with joy.

The Wise Men went to the house.
There they saw the child with his mother Mary.
They bowed down and worshiped him.
Then they opened their treasures.
They gave him gold, incense and myrrh.

God warned them in a dream
not to go back to Herod.
So they returned on a different road.

The Escape to Egypt

Matthew 2

When the Wise Men had left,
an angel appeared to Joseph in a dream.
"Get up!" the angel said. "Take the child
and his mother and escape to Egypt.
Stay there until I tell you to come back.
Herod wants to kill him."

Joseph got up. During the night, he left for Egypt with the child and his mother Mary. They stayed there until King Herod died.

The Boy Jesus at the Temple

Luke 2

Every year Jesus' parents went
to Jerusalem for the Passover Feast.
When he was 12 years old, they went
to the Feast as usual. After the Feast
was over, his parents left to go home.
Jesus stayed behind in Jerusalem.

But they were not aware of it. They thought he was somewhere in their group. So they traveled on for a day. Then they began to look for him among their friends. They did not find him. So they went back to Jerusalem to look for him.

After three days they found him in
the temple. He was sitting with the teachers,
listening to them and asking them questions.
Everyone who heard him was amazed
at how much he understood.
They also were amazed at his answers.

When his parents saw him, they were amazed.
His mother said, "Why have you treated us like
this? Your father and I have been worried about
you. We have been looking for you everywhere."
"Why were you looking for me?" he asked.
"Didn't you know I had to be in my Father's house?"
But they did not understand what he meant.

Then he went back to Nazareth with them, and he obeyed them. Jesus became wiser and stronger. He became more pleasing to God and to people.

John the Baptist

Matthew 3; Mark 1

John the Baptist preached in the desert.
People went to him from all of Judea.
John baptized them in the Jordan River.

John's clothes were made of camel's hair.
He had a leather belt around his waist.
His food was locusts and wild honey.
John said, "I baptize you with water.
But after me, one will come who is
more powerful than I am.
I'm not fit to carry his sandals.
He will baptize you with the Holy Spirit."

Jesus Is Baptized

Matthew 3

Jesus came to the Jordan River.
He wanted to be baptized by John.

As soon as Jesus was baptized,
he came up out of the water.
At that moment heaven was opened.
Jesus saw the Spirit of God
coming down on him like a dove.
A voice from heaven said,
"This is my Son, and I love him.
I am very pleased with him."

Jesus Calls the Disciples

Matthew 4; Mark 2

One day Jesus was walking
beside the Sea of Galilee.
He saw Simon Peter and his brother Andrew.
They were throwing a net into the lake.
They were fishermen.
"Come. Follow me," Jesus said.
"I will make you fishers of people."
At once they left their nets and followed him.

Later, Jesus saw two other brothers, James and John.
They were in a boat with their father.
As they were preparing their nets,
Jesus called them. Right away they left
the boat and their father and followed Jesus.

Once again Jesus went out beside the sea. As he walked along he saw Levi sitting at the tax collector's booth. "Follow me," Jesus told him. Levi got up and followed him.

Jesus Changes Water to Wine
John 2

A wedding took place at Cana.
Jesus' mother was there.
Jesus and his disciples were
also invited to the wedding.

When the wine was gone, Jesus' mother said to him,
"They have no more wine."
His mother said to the servants,
"Do what he tells you."
Six stone water jars stood nearby.
Jesus said to the servants, "Fill the jars with water."
So they filled them to the top.

He told them, "Now dip some out.
Take it to the person in charge of the dinner."
The person in charge tasted the water that
had been turned into wine.
He called the groom to one side. He said,
"You have saved the best wine until now."
That was the first of Jesus' miraculous signs.

Jesus Teaches About Praying

Matthew 5 — 6

Jesus went up on a mountainside and sat down.
His disciples came to him.
Then he began to teach them.
He said, "This is how you should pray.

Our Father in heaven, may your name be
    honored.
May your kingdom come.
May what you want to happen be done
  on earth as it is done in heaven.
Give us today our daily bread.
Forgive us our sins, just as we also have
  forgiven those who sin against us.
Keep us from sin when we are tempted.
Save us from the evil one."

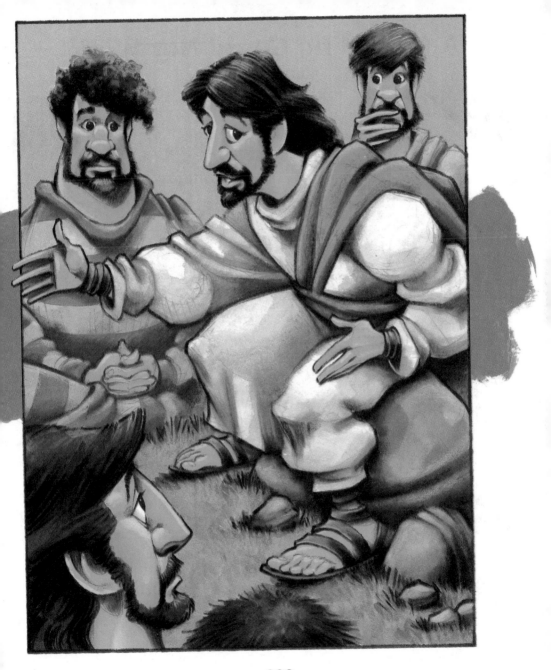

A Man Who Could Not Walk

Mark 2; Luke 5

One day Jesus was teaching.
Some men came carrying a man who could not walk.
But they could not get him
close to Jesus because of the crowd.

They made a hole in the roof above Jesus.
Then they lowered the man through it on a mat.
They lowered him into the middle of the crowd,
  right in front of Jesus.

When Jesus saw they had faith, he said to the man who could not walk, "Get up. Take your mat and go home."

Right away, the man stood up.
He took his mat and went home praising God.
All the people were amazed. They praised God
and said, "We have never seen anything like this!"

Jesus Calms the Storm

Matthew 8; Mark 4; Luke 8

One day Jesus said to his disciples,
"Let's go over to the other side of the lake."

As they sailed, a storm came
on the lake. Waves crashed
over the boat.
It was about to sink.
But Jesus was sleeping.

Jesus got up and ordered the wind and waves to stop. He said, "Quiet! Be still!"
The wind died down. It was completely calm.

He said to his disciples, "Why are you so afraid? Don't you have any faith?"

They were terrified. They asked each other, "Who is this?
Even the wind and waves obey him!"

A Girl Who Died

Matthew 9; Mark 5

A man named Jairus came. He begged Jesus,
"My daughter has just died.
But come and place your hand on her.
Then she will live again."
Jesus went with him.

They came to Jairus' home. People were crying.
Jesus went inside. He said,
"The child is not dead. She is only sleeping."
But they laughed at him.

He made them go outside. He took
the child's father and mother in where
the child was. He took her by
the hand. He said, "Little girl, get up!"

Right away she stood up and walked around.
They were totally amazed at this.

Jesus Feeds 5,000

Matthew 14; Luke 9; John 6

Jesus saw a large crowd.
He felt deep concern for them.
He healed their sick people.

Late in the afternoon the disciples came to him.
They said, "Send the crowd away.
They can go find food. There is nothing here."
Jesus replied, "They don't need to go away.
You give them something to eat."

Andrew spoke up,
"Here is a boy."

"He has five loaves of bread. He also has
two small fish. But how far will that go?"

314

Jesus told the people to sit on the grass. He took the loaves and the fishes. He gave thanks. He broke them into pieces. He gave them to the disciples to set in front of the people.

When all of them had enough to eat,
Jesus spoke, "Gather the leftover pieces.
Don't waste anything."

The disciples picked up 12 baskets of leftover pieces. The number of men who ate was about 5,000.
Women and children also ate.

Jesus Walks on Water

Matthew 14; Mark 6; John 6

Jesus made the disciples get into the boat. He had them go ahead of him to Bethsaida. He went up on a mountainside to pray.

When evening came, the boat was in the middle of the lake. Jesus was alone on land.
He saw the disciples pulling hard on the oars. The wind was blowing against them.

Jesus went out to the disciples. He walked on the lake.
They saw him walking on the lake.
They thought he was a ghost. They were terrified.

Right away he said,
"Be brave! It is I. Don't be afraid."

"Lord, is it you?" Peter asked. "Tell me to come to you on the water."

"Come," Jesus said.

So Peter got out of the boat. He walked on the water to Jesus.

But when he saw the wind, he was afraid.

He began to sink. He cried, "Lord! Save me!"

Right away Jesus reached out his hand and caught him.

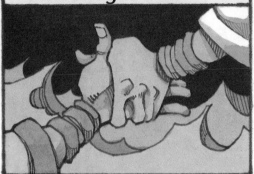

When they climbed into the boat, the wind died down.

Then those in the boat worshiped Jesus. They said, "You really are the Son of God."

Jesus told this story to the people:

The Good Samaritan
Luke 10

A man was going from Jerusalem to Jericho. Robbers attacked him.

They stripped off his clothes and beat him. Then they went away, leaving him almost dead.

A priest happened to be going down that same road. When he saw the man, he passed by on the other side.

A Levite passed by on the other side too.

But a Samaritan came and felt sorry for the man. He went to him and poured olive oil and wine on his wounds. He put the man on his own donkey, took him to an inn and took care of him.

The next day he gave two silver coins to the owner of the inn. "Take care of him," he said. "When I return, I will pay you for any extra expense."

Jesus said, "Which of the three
do you think was a neighbor
to the man who was attacked?"
The authority on the law replied,
"The one who felt sorry for him."
Jesus told him,
"Go and do as he did."

At Mary and Martha's Home

Luke 10

Jesus came to a village where a woman named
Martha lived. She welcomed him into her home.

She had a sister named Mary. Mary sat at the Lord's feet listening to what he said.

But Martha was busy with all
the things that had to be done.

She came to Jesus and said, "My sister
has left me to do the work by myself.
Don't you care?
Tell her to help me!

"Martha, Martha," the Lord answered.
"You are worried and upset about many things.
But only one thing is needed.
Mary has chosen what is better.
And it will not be taken away from her."

Jesus Raises Lazarus

John 11

Mary and Martha's brother Lazarus was sick.
So the sisters sent a message to Jesus.
"Lord," they told him, "The one you love is sick."

Jesus loved Martha and Mary and Lazarus.
But after he heard Lazarus was sick,
he stayed where he was for two more days.
Then he said to his disciples,
"Lazarus is dead. But let us go to him."

When Jesus arrived, he found out that Lazarus
had already been in the tomb for four days.
Many Jews had come to Martha
and Mary to comfort them.
"Where have you put him?" Jesus asked.
"Come and see, Lord," they replied.
Jesus sobbed. Then the Jews said,
"See how much he loved him!"

Jesus came to the tomb. It was a cave with a stone in front. "Take away the stone," he said.

"Lord," said Martha, "by this time there is a bad smell. Lazarus has been in the tomb for 4 days."

Then Jesus said, "Didn't I tell you that if you believed, you would see God's glory?"

So they took away the stone.

Jesus called in a loud voice, "Lazarus, come out!"
The dead man came out. His hands and feet
were wrapped with strips of linen. A cloth was
around his face. Jesus said to them,
"Take off the clothes he was buried in
and let him go." Many of the Jews who
had come to visit Mary saw what Jesus did.
So they put their faith in him.

339

The Story of the Lost Sheep

Luke 15

Jesus told a story. He said:
Suppose one of you has 100 sheep and loses
one of them. Won't he leave the 99 in the
open country? Won't he go and look
for the one lost sheep until he finds it?
When he finds it, he will joyfully put it
on his shoulders and go home.
Then he will call his friends and neighbors.

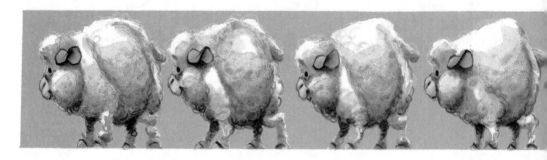

He will say, "Be joyful with me.
I have found my lost sheep."
I tell you, it will be the same in heaven.
There will be great joy when one sinner
turns away from sin. Yes, there will be
more joy than for 99 godly people who
do not need to turn away from their sins.

The Story of the Lost Coin
Luke 15

Jesus told a story:
Suppose a woman has ten silver coins
and loses one. She will light a lamp and
sweep the house. She will search carefully
until she finds the coin.

And when she finds it,
she will call her friends
and neighbors. She will say,
"Be joyful with me.
I have found my lost coin."
I tell you, it is the same
in heaven. There is joy
in heaven over one sinner
who turns away from sin.

343

The Story of the Lost Son

Luke 15

Jesus told a story:
A man had two sons. The younger son
spoke to his father. He said, "Father,
give me my share of the family property."
So the father divided his
property between his two sons.

Not long after that, the younger son packed up all he had. He left for a country far away. There he wasted his money on wild living.

He spent everything he had. He went to work
for someone who sent him to feed pigs.
He wanted to fill his stomach with the food
the pigs were eating. But no one gave him
anything.

Then he began to think. He said,
"How many of my father's hired workers
have more than enough food! But here I am
dying from hunger."
So he got up and went to his father.

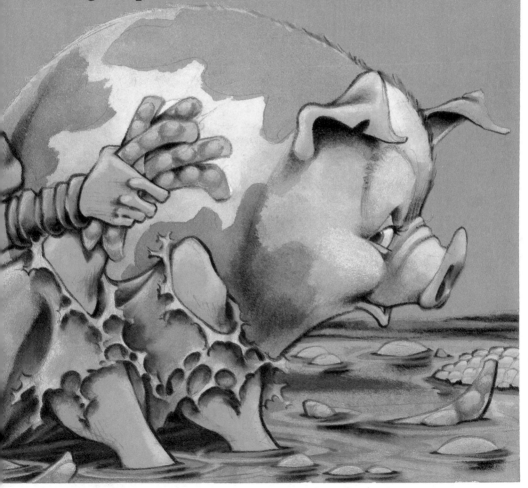

While the son was still a long way off, his father saw him.
He was filled with tender love for his son. He ran to him.
He threw his arms around him and kissed him.

The son said, "Father, I have sinned. I am no longer fit to be called your son."

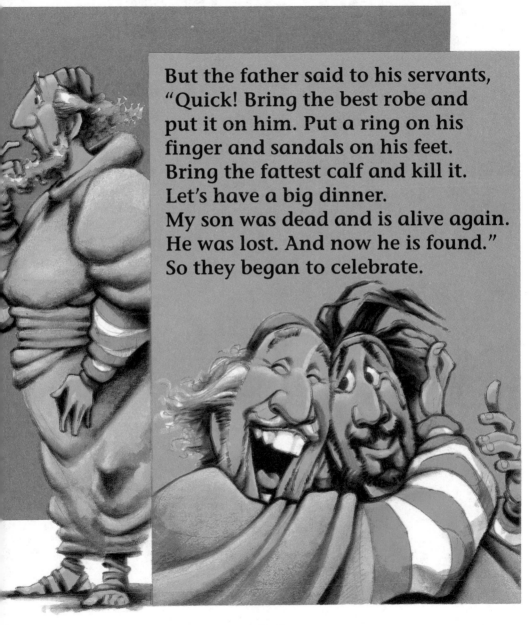

But the father said to his servants,
"Quick! Bring the best robe and
put it on him. Put a ring on his
finger and sandals on his feet.
Bring the fattest calf and kill it.
Let's have a big dinner.
My son was dead and is alive again.
He was lost. And now he is found."
So they began to celebrate.

Jesus Heals Ten Men

Luke 17

As Jesus was going into a village, ten men met him. They had a skin disease. They called out, "Jesus! Master! Have pity on us!"

Jesus saw them and said, "Go. Show yourselves to the priests." While they were on their way, they were healed.

When one of them saw that he was healed,
he came back. He praised God in a loud voice.
He threw himself at Jesus' feet and thanked him.

Jesus asked, "Weren't all ten healed?
Where are the other nine?"
Then Jesus said to him, "Get up and go.
Your faith has healed you."

Jesus and the Children

Matthew 19; Mark 10; Luke 18

Some people brought little children
to Jesus. They wanted him to place
his hands on the children and pray for them.
The disciples told the people to stop.
But Jesus asked the children to come to him.
"Let the little children come to me," he said.
"Don't keep them away.
God's kingdom belongs to people like them."
Then he took the children in his arms.
He put his hands on them and blessed them.

A Very Short Man

Luke 19

Zacchaeus was a tax collector and was very rich. He wanted to see Jesus. But he was a short man. He could not see Jesus because of the crowd.

So Zacchaeus ran and climbed
a tree. Jesus reached the spot
where Zacchaeus was and said,
"Zacchaeus, come down at once.
I must stay at your house today."
So Zacchaeus came down and
welcomed him gladly.

Jesus Enters Jerusalem

Matthew 21; Mark 11; Luke 19

As they approached Jerusalem, Jesus sent out two disciples. He said, "Go to the village ahead of you. As soon as you get there, you will find a donkey's colt tied up. Untie it and bring it here. If anyone says anything to you, tell him the Lord needs it."
The disciples went and did what Jesus told them. They found a colt in the street.
It was tied at a doorway. They untied it.
Some people asked, "What are you doing?"
They answered as Jesus had told them to.
So the people let them go.

The disciples brought the colt to Jesus.
They threw their coats over it and put
Jesus on it. A very large crowd
spread their coats on the road.

Others spread branches they had cut in the fields. The whole crowd began to praise God with joy. They shouted, "Hosanna! Blessed is the one who comes in the name of the Lord! Hosanna in the highest heaven!"

Mary Pours Perfume

John 12

A dinner was given to honor Jesus.
Martha served the food. Lazarus was among
those at the table with Jesus.
Then Mary took an expensive perfume.

She poured the perfume on Jesus' feet
and wiped them with her hair.
The house was filled with
the sweet smell of the perfume.

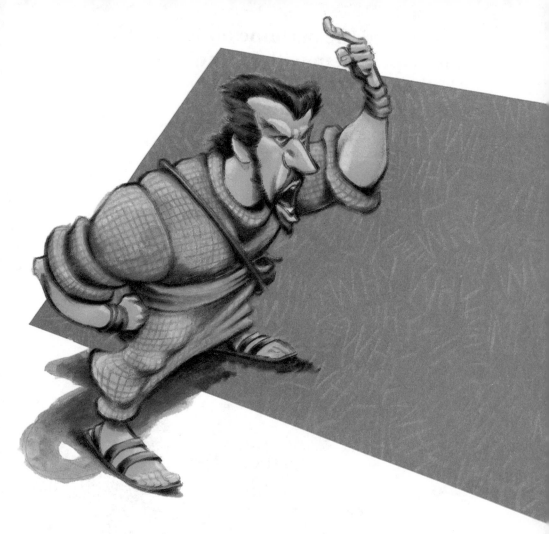

Judas Iscariot didn't like what Mary did.
Judas said, "Why wasn't this perfume sold
and the money given to the poor?"
He didn't say this because he cared about the poor.
He said it because he was a thief.

"Leave her alone," Jesus replied. "The perfume was meant for the day I am buried. You will always have poor people. But you won't always have me."

Jesus Washes the Disciples' Feet

John 13

It was just before the Passover Feast.
The evening meal was being served.
So Jesus got up from the meal.
He wrapped a towel around his waist.

He poured water into a large bowl.
He began to wash his disciples' feet.
He dried them with the towel
that was wrapped around him.

"Do you understand what I have done for you?" he asked them. "I, your Lord and Teacher, have washed your feet. So you also should wash one another's feet. I have given you an example. You should do as I have done. Now you know these things. You will be blessed if you do them."

The Lord's Supper

Matthew 26; Mark 14

The day came to celebrate the Passover Feast.
Jesus sent out two of his disciples.
He told them, "Go into the city.
A man carrying a jar of water will meet you.
Follow him. He will show you a large
upstairs room. Prepare for us to eat there."

The disciples went into the city.
They found things just as Jesus had told them.
So they prepared the Passover meal.
When evening came,
Jesus arrived with the Twelve.

While they were eating,
Jesus took bread.
He gave thanks and broke it.
He handed it to his disciples
and said, "Take it. This is my body."

Then he took the cup. He gave thanks and handed it to them. All of them drank from it.

"This is my blood poured out to forgive the sins of many," he said. Then they sang a hymn and went out to the Mount of Olives.

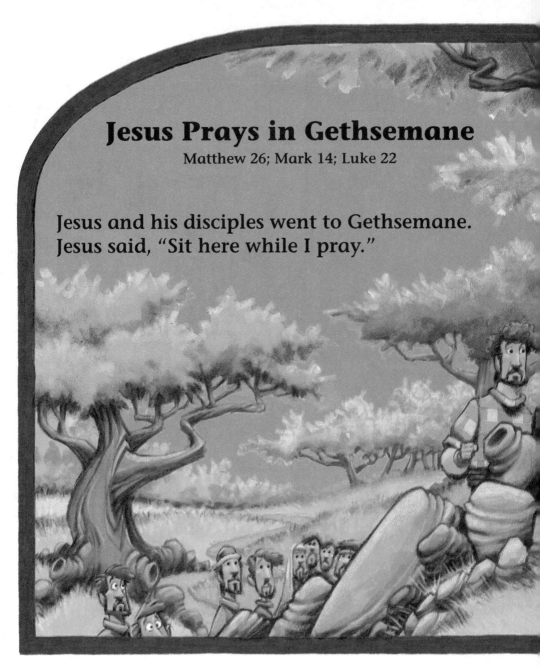

Jesus Prays in Gethsemane

Matthew 26; Mark 14; Luke 22

Jesus and his disciples went to Gethsemane. Jesus said, "Sit here while I pray."

He took Peter, James and John along with him.
He got down on his knees and prayed, "Father,
if you are willing, take this cup away from me.
But do what you want, not what I want."
An angel from heaven appeared
to Jesus and gave him strength.

He got up from prayer and went back to the disciples. He found them sleeping. "Why are you sleeping," he asked. "Get up! Pray that you won't fall into sin when you are tempted." Once more Jesus went away and prayed the same thing. Then he came back. Again he found them sleeping.

So he left them. For the third time he prayed.
He returned to the disciples and said,
"Are you still sleeping? Look! The hour is near.
The Son of Man is about to be handed
over to sinners. Get up! Let us go!
Here comes the one who is handing me over!"

Jesus Is Arrested

Matthew 26; Mark 14; Luke 22; John 18

Jesus had finished praying. He and his disciples went into a grove of olive trees. Judas knew the place. Jesus had often been in that place.

So Judas came, guiding a group of soldiers. They were carrying torches and weapons.

Jesus asked them, "Who is it that you want?"
"Jesus of Nazareth," they replied.
"I am he," Jesus said.

Judas went to Jesus. He said, "Greetings, Rabbi!" And he kissed him. Jesus asked him, "Judas, are you handing over the Son of Man with a kiss?" Peter had a sword and pulled it out. He cut off a servant's right ear. Jesus commanded Peter, "Put your sword away!" And he touched the man's ear and healed him.

Then the soldiers arrested Jesus. They tied him up. All the disciples left and ran away.

Jesus Goes to Pilate

Matthew 27; Mark 15

Early in the morning, the priests, the elders and the whole Sanhedrin made a decision. They tied Jesus up. Then they handed him over to Pilate.

"Are you the king of the Jews?" asked Pilate.
"Yes. It is just as you say," Jesus replied.

It was the practice at the Passover Feast to let one prisoner go free. The people could choose the one they wanted. Pilate asked, "Which one do you want me to set free? Barabbas? Or Jesus?"

"Barabbas," they answered.

"What should I do with Jesus?" Pilate asked.
They all answered, "Crucify him!"
"Why? What wrong has he done?" asked Pilate.
But they shouted even louder, "Crucify him!"

Pilate saw that he wasn't getting anywhere.
So he took water and washed
his hands in front of the crowd.
"I am not guilty of this man's death," he said.

Pilate let Barabbas
go free. But he had
Jesus whipped.
Then he handed him
over to be nailed
to a cross.

I Don't Know Him

Mark 14; Luke 22

Peter was in the courtyard. Soldiers started a fire. Then they sat down. Peter sat down with them.

A servant came by. She saw Peter.
"You were with Jesus," she said.
But Peter said he had not been with him.
"I don't know him," he said.

A little later someone else saw Peter. "You are one of them," he said. "No," Peter replied. "I'm not!"

After a little while, those standing nearby said to Peter, "You must be one of them."

Peter replied,
"I don't know what
you're talking about!"
Just as he was speaking
the rooster crowed.

The Lord turned and looked at Peter.
Then Peter remembered what Jesus had said.
"The rooster will crow. Before it does, you will
say three times that you don't know me."
Peter broke down and sobbed.

Jesus Dies

Matthew 27; Luke 23; John 19

Jesus had to carry his cross to a place called The Skull. There the soldiers nailed him to the cross.

Jesus said, "Father, forgive them.
They don't know what they are doing."
A written sign above him read:
This is Jesus, The King of the Jews.
Two robbers were crucified with him.
One was on his right and one on his left.
For three hours, the land was covered
with darkness. Jesus cried out in a
loud voice, "My God, my God,
why have you deserted me?"
After Jesus cried out again,
he bowed his head and died.

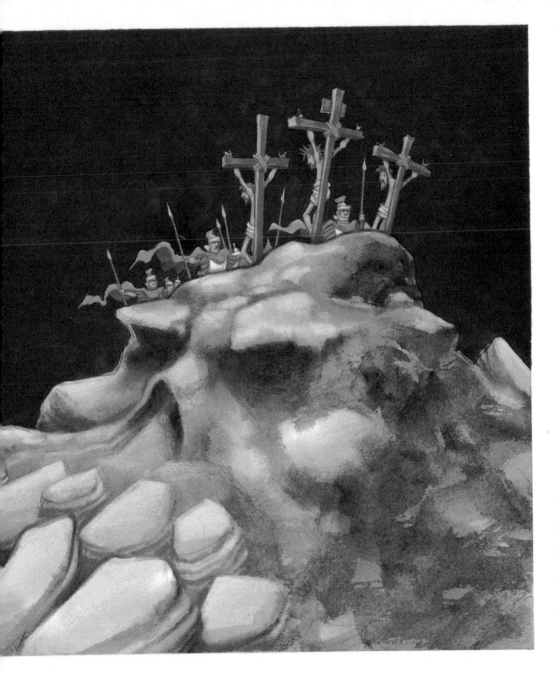

Jesus Is Buried

Matthew 27

As evening approached, a rich man went to Pilate.
His name was Joseph. He asked for Jesus' body.
Pilate ordered that it be given to him.
Joseph took the body and wrapped it in a
clean linen cloth. He placed it in his own new tomb.

He rolled a big stone in front of the tomb. Then he went away. Pilate put a seal on the stone and placed some guards on duty.

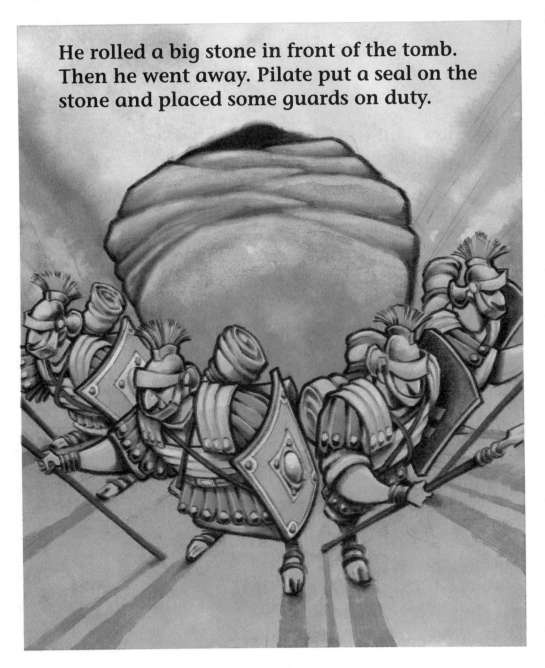

The Tomb Is Empty

Matthew 28; Mark 16; John 20

It was dawn on the first day of the week.
Mary Magdalene and the other Mary
went to look at the tomb.
They saw that the stone had been rolled
away. They entered the tomb. As they did,
they saw an angel dressed in a white robe.

The angel said to the women, "Don't be
afraid. I know you are looking for Jesus.
He is not here! He has risen, just as he said!
Go! Tell his disciples and Peter."
So the women hurried away
from the tomb. They were afraid,
but they were filled with joy.
They ran to tell the disciples.

Jesus Appears to His Disciples

Luke 24; John 20

On the evening of the first day of the week, the disciples were together. They had locked the doors because they were afraid of the Jews. Jesus came in and stood among them. He said, "May peace be with you!"

Then he showed them his hands and his side.
The disciples were very happy
when they saw the Lord.
Jesus asked them, "Do you have anything to eat?"
They gave him a piece of cooked fish.
He took it and ate it in front of them.

Jesus Goes Up to Heaven

Acts 1

After his death, Jesus appeared to his
disciples over a period of 40 days.
After this, he was taken up to heaven.
They watched until a cloud hid
him from sight.

While he was going up, they kept on looking at the sky. Suddenly two men dressed in white clothing stood beside them. They said, "Why do you stand here looking at the sky? Jesus has been taken away from you into heaven. But he will come back in the same way you saw him go." So the apostles returned to Jerusalem.

The Holy Spirit Comes

Acts 2

The day of Pentecost came. The believers all gathered in one place. Suddenly a sound came from heaven. It was like a strong wind. It filled the whole house where they were sitting.

They saw tongues of fire on each of them.
They were filled with the Holy Spirit.
They began to speak in languages
they had not known before.

Jews from every country heard the believers
speaking in their own language. The crowd
was amazed. They asked, "What does this mean?"
But some people made fun of the believers.
"They've had too much wine!" they said.
Then Peter stood up. In a loud voice he said,
"God raised Jesus back to life. We are witnesses
of this. Turn away from sin and be baptized."
About 3,000 people joined the believers that day.

407

Peter Heals a Beggar

Acts 3

One day Peter and John were going up to the
temple. A man unable to walk was being
carried to the temple gate called Beautiful.
Every day someone put him near the gate.
He would beg from people going into the temple.

He saw Peter and John. So he asked them for money. Peter looked straight at him, and so did John. Then Peter said, "Look at us! I don't have any silver or gold. But I'll give you what I have. In the name of Jesus Christ, get up and walk." Then Peter took him by the right hand and helped him up.

At once the man's feet and ankles became strong.
He jumped to his feet and began to walk.
He went with Peter and John into the temple.
He walked and jumped and praised God.
All the people were filled with wonder.

The Man From Ethiopia

Acts 8

An angel of the Lord spoke to Philip, "Go south to the desert road that goes down from Jerusalem to Gaza."

On his way he met an Ethiopian official.
The man had an important position. He was in
charge of all the wealth of the queen of Ethiopia.
He had gone to Jerusalem to worship.
On his way home he was sitting in his chariot.
He was reading the book of Isaiah.

Philip heard the man reading. "Do you understand what you're reading?" Philip asked. "How can I?" he said. "I need someone to explain it." He invited Philip to come up and sit with him. Then Philip told him the good news about Jesus.

As they traveled along the road,
they came to some water. The official said,
"Look! Here is water!
Why shouldn't I be baptized?"
Then both Philip and the official went down
into the water. Philip baptized him.

Saul Believes

Acts 9

Saul wanted to find men and women
who belonged to Jesus. He wanted
to take them as prisoners to Jerusalem.

On his journey, Saul approached Damascus. Suddenly a light from heaven flashed around him. He fell to the ground. He heard a voice say to him, "Saul! Saul! Why are you opposing me?" "Who are you, Lord?" Saul asked.

"I am Jesus," he replied. "I am the one you
are opposing. Now get up and go into the city.
There you will be told what you must do."
The men traveling with Saul weren't able to speak.
They heard the sound. But they didn't see anyone.

Saul got up from the ground. He opened his eyes,
but he couldn't see. So the men led him
by the hand into Damascus.
For three days he was blind.

In Damascus there was a believer named Ananias.
The Lord called to him in a vision, "Ananias!
Go to the house of Judas on Straight Street.
Ask for a man named Saul. He is praying."

Then Ananias went to the house. He placed his hands on Saul. "Brother Saul," he said, "you saw Jesus. He has sent me so that you will be able to see again. You will be filled with the Holy Spirit."

Right away something like scales fell from Saul's eyes. And he could see again. He got up and was baptized.

Saul in Damascus

Acts 9

Saul spent several days
with the believers
in Damascus.
He began to preach that
Jesus is the Son of God.
All who heard him were
amazed. They asked,
"Isn't he the man who
caused great trouble
in Jerusalem for those
who worship Jesus?"
After many days, the
Jews planned to kill Saul.
But he learned of their plan.
Day and night they
watched the city
gates closely in order
to kill him.

But his followers helped him escape by night. They lowered him in a basket through an opening in the wall.

Paul and Silas in Prison

Acts 13; 16

Some men in Philippi grabbed Saul, who
was also known as Paul, and Silas.
Paul and Silas were thrown into prison.
The jailer was commanded to guard them carefully.

424

He put them deep inside the prison.
He fastened their feet so they couldn't
get away. About midnight Paul and
Silas were praying and singing to God.
The prisoners were listening to them.

Suddenly there was a powerful earthquake.
It shook the prison from the top to bottom.
All the prison doors flew open.
Everybody's chains came loose.

The jailer woke up.
He saw the prison doors were open.
He pulled out his sword to kill himself.
He thought the prisoners had escaped.
"Don't harm yourself!" Paul shouted.
"We're all here!"

The jailer rushed in, shaking with fear.
He fell down in front of Paul and Silas.
Then he brought them out.
He asked, "Sirs, what must I do to be saved?"
They replied, "Believe in the Lord Jesus.
Then you and your family will be saved."

Right away he and all his family were baptized.
The jailer brought Paul and Silas into his house.
He set a meal in front of them.
He and his whole family were filled with joy.
They had become believers in God.

Paul Sails for Rome

Acts 27

Paul and some other prisoners were put on board a ship sailing for Rome. Before very long, the ship was caught by a storm. It had the force of a hurricane.

The men tied ropes under
the ship to hold it together.
They were afraid it would
get stuck on sandbars.
They lowered the sea anchor
and let the ship be driven along.

The storm was terrible. On the 14th night the sailors had a feeling that they were approaching land. They were afraid the ship would crash against the rocks. They dropped four anchors from the back of the ship. They prayed that daylight would come.

Just before dawn Paul tried to get them to eat. "For the last 14 days," he said, "you have gone without food. I am asking you to eat some food. You need it to live. Not one of you will lose a single hair from your head."
All of them were filled with hope. So they ate.

When daylight came, they saw a sandy beach.
They decided to run the ship onto the beach.
But the ship hit a sandbar and wouldn't move.

The commander ordered those who could swim to jump overboard and swim to land. The rest were supposed to get there on pieces of the ship. That is how everyone reached land safely.

Jesus Is Coming

Revelation 21 — 22

I heard a loud voice. It said,
"Now God makes his home
with human beings.
He will live with them.
They will be his people.
And God himself will
be with them and be
their God.